Divorce Is Worse than Death

Stanley McCluskey

DEDICATION

To the families and friends that have been affected by divorce, especially "Jill" for teaching me that "divorce is worse than death"…and to my family.

CONTENTS

ACKNOWLEDGMENTS

My profound thanks and gratitude go to the following people: first and foremost, the wonderful people who were willing to be vulnerable and share their divorce stories with me; Charlene Day, who helped jumpstart my dream making me believe that I had a book inside of me to write; Karen Roberts for giving me the push to start writing and serving as my encourager; Pearl Matibe, Alka Bromiley, Chris Jordan, Clyde Middleton, Dominique Brightmon, Haki Ammi, Tammy Wylie, Rick Estberg, Mia Redrick, Claudio Toyama, Jeff Davis, John L. Nicodemus, and Brian J. Olds for their entrepreneurial spirit that helped me aim higher; Sherry Kuiper, Yvonne Foster, Rabbi Irv Elson, Tatyana Bunich, John Logan, Brandy McCluskey, Brittany McCluskey Nickodemus and Jacob Nickodemus for their help; Michele Chynoweth who served as my editor, friend, and mentor making this book possible through her book coaching and most of all her encouragement which helped me to continue to move forward; and last but certainly not least, to my wife, Jennifer for her unwavering support for this writing project. Praise be to God and my savior Jesus Christ for allowing me to get to this point in my life and equipping me with wonderful and talented family and friends.

FOREWORD

"Divorce is probably as painful as death." –William Shatner, Actor

For some people, divorce is worse than death. However, we live in a time when many perceive that getting a divorce is trivial. The American Psychological Association website states that forty to fifty percent of married couples in the United States divorce. Due to the frequency of divorce many people now compare divorcing a spouse to the experience of breaking up with a boyfriend or girlfriend from high school.

It seems that many of our friends and family members tend to go through the divorce process with the mindset that getting a divorce is "no big deal." This nonchalant attitude leaves many people who are experiencing great pain from divorce believing that something is wrong with them personally since their divorce is not trivial and is a *huge* deal—their divorces have left them feeling physically sick, mentally drained and emotionally raw, their days filled with tears, followed by sleepless nights—and in some cases, like they would rather die.

Before we can discuss the effects of divorce we need to go back to the beginning—what may have been the happiest day of one's life: the wedding day. A person may have spent his or her entire life searching for that special person who would someday be chosen as a soulmate for life. In some cases that soulmate might have been a high school sweetheart, the only person he or she ever dated. For some the search may go on for years with heartbreak after heartbreak until the perfect spouse is found. In most situations both partners seemingly discovered their soulmates, and each made a conscious decision to choose each other for life, signing a marriage license creating a civil "marriage contract" and becoming joined as one in holy matrimony. This is the happiest day of their lives!

In most cases, the wedding of choice in the United States is a traditional one where numerous guests attend a ceremony and then a reception afterward. Months of planning go into searching for the perfect wedding venue, dress, caterer, music, and so many other items required to make the day special. The bride and groom join their guests at the reception where a great celebration occurs with feasting and dancing in honor of the union of these two beautiful and happy people filled with love for each other. Today they are the king and queen of their newly formed "kingdom."

Fast forward several years later to when the king and queen discover that their kingdom is falling apart and laying in shambles with the marriage coming to an end. In some cases there may have been signs that the marriage was crumbling prior to one partner deciding to call it quits. In other cases, there are no warning signs when one partner surprises the other by walking out of the marriage leaving him or her in shock. There are numerous scenarios that can be reviewed and discussed on the breakup of a marriage, but for the most part the result is still the same—the end of a marriage, the death of a dream. Two people who at one time could not have imagined spending their lives apart will now go their separate ways. And most of the time, one or more people are left experiencing a broken heart.

Famous supermodel Christie Brinkley has been quoted as saying, "I'd rather have a broken arm than a broken heart." She is by far not alone in this sentiment.

When people go through a breakup of a marriage or romantic relationship, they often state that their hearts are broken. Some will actually experience a pain in their chests that causes them to actually feel like their heart is breaking.

With a broken heart, it is hard to tell how bad the break is because it is hard to quantify it—there are no medical devices available to provide a visual representation of a broken heart. However, there are several assessment tests that can be administered to people experiencing a loss and based on those answers, the medical professional can draft a list of questions that can be used to at least understand the break, even though it can't be measured.

But before anyone can start healing from a physical or internal injury, the patient must obviously first seek out medical treatment. When someone breaks a bone in his or her body, he or she will usually seek medical attention immediately based on the severity of the break. But a person that experiences a heart break from the loss of a loved one through death or divorce may not realize the urgent need for medical counseling. In fact, most people seek help from well-meaning friends who are as ill-equipped to provide valid assistance with a broken heart as they would be with a broken bone.

I remember when I crashed my motorcycle and broke my leg. It happened around seven o'clock on a cool spring morning in March 2017 as I was riding "Sporty," my Harley Davidson Sportster motorcycle to work. I had just merged into rush hour, stop-and-go traffic on the southbound lane of Interstate-295, known as the Baltimore-Washington (B-W) Parkway. I took my eyes off the car in front me for a second and it suddenly stopped in front of me. I overreacted by applying the brakes too hard causing Sporty and me to land in separate lanes, blocking rush hour traffic and causing the B-W Parkway to become a real "parkway." I was laying on my back unable to stand, but worst of all, I was unable to complete a damage assessment of Sporty.

That's when an "angel" appeared, an Airman who stopped her car and rushed to my side to check on me. I told her I was ok but asked her to check on Sporty and move my baby to the shoulder of the road. She complied, which not only made me happy but cleared up one lane of traffic making the morning commuters happy too. She then rushed back over to me and said, "Good news! Your motorcycle is ok. Your baby's not hurt."

"Thank you, sweet Jesus!" I replied. I knew if Sporty was damaged my wife would never allow me to purchase a replacement.

I wanted to stay with Sporty and had no desire to go to the hospital but found that I had no choice. The paramedics who were first on the scene didn't see any visible signs of injury so they attempted to help me stand but I quickly collapsed to the ground, unable to bear any weight on my leg.

The paramedics transported me to the local hospital Emergency Room (ER) where the doctor on call immediately ordered an X-ray for my damaged leg which clearly showed it was broken. I was given a brace and medication and was referred to an orthopedic specialist who ordered an MRI to obtain a clearer picture of the actual damage. The MRI revealed that not only did I break my leg but had damaged my ACL as well. His ability to have a picture of my injury allowed him to view the seriousness of it and schedule me for surgery to correct the damage.

People experiencing a broken heart don't always realize the immobilizing nature of it. They tend to go about their daily routines at home and work believing there is nothing wrong while they are, in reality, consumed with the thoughts and feelings resulting from the loss they are facing.

People need time to heal whether experiencing a physical break or a heart break, but the time for healing may vary greatly between individuals who may experience similar breaks or break ups. In any healing situation, it is very helpful for a medical professional to provide an approximate recovery date to help manage expectations. Anyone who encounters a broken bone or broken heart wants to know, "when will I heal?" It is, of course, much easier to approximate the recovery date for a broken bone because there is tangible evidence that can be measured. No one can truly give a recovery date for a broken heart. And people all heal differently.

When I had my accident and realized that my leg was broken, I remembered a co-worker who had recently broken her leg and how quickly she healed. She was able to return to work in less than a week after her accident and was able to have a full recovery in seven weeks. I was expecting the same rapid recovery until I was presented with the results of my MRI and found out I would need surgery, would be off from work for seven weeks and would be in a wheelchair for three months before I could even start physical therapy. As devastating as my prognosis was, I was still glad that my doctor was able to use technology to show me the severity of the break. Without quantitative measurements, I would have been left wondering, *what is wrong with me? Why was my co-worker able to heal in seven weeks while it would take me seven months?* The quantitative measures helped me understand that there was nothing wrong with me except that my leg was more badly damaged compared to my coworker's.

Having my recovery date in mind was a psychological boost as I was healing. Once I started working with a physical therapy team, I was able to slowly make progress in gaining more motion and flexibility in my leg. The physical therapy team would perform periodic evaluations where they would use tools to measure my flexibility and motion. For me the measurements provided a metric that my mobility was slowly returning, providing an extra psychological boost.

Someone who is faced with a broken heart does not have the luxury of having therapists literally measure the broken heart and show metrics for healing, nor give them any tangible timeline. All they can offer is hope that their pain will eventually diminish.

While it is easy to define pain as "physical suffering or discomfort caused by illness or injury," describing the pain level caused by a physical or psychological injury can be hard to describe or articulate, especially when due to a broken heart. If you ask someone to describe his or her pain based on a scale of one to ten where one is the minimum amount and ten is the maximum, you will get a wide range of responses. People have various tolerance levels.

Describing the levels of pain was one of the most frustrating tasks I had to deal with while I was in the hospital recovering from my leg surgery. During my recovery I found myself in excruciating pain and when the nurse on duty would ask me to describe my pain level from one to ten, I personally didn't have a clue how to respond. The nurse on duty would tell me that I was the only one that could really articulate my pain level. That's when I asked myself, *was my pain at a five where ten is the pain level that a woman experiences during childbirth?* I finally decided to come up with my own pain gauge and decided that my pain was an eight. I realized quickly that the pain level determined whether or not I would get medication to help assuage the pain that I was experiencing.

Someone experiencing the pain of loss may find it particularly hard to articulate the pain on a scale from one to ten. But just like I was the only one who could articulate my own pain, you are the only one who can articulate your pain level.

There is no "one-divorce fits all" theory, diagnosis or remedy for a broken heart. Each is unique. There are those who can walk away from a divorce with a "sprained" heart while others' hearts are crushed or mangled. There are some who take several days to heal, many that take several weeks or months, and others who take years.

No one should ever be able to tell you how you should feel. You're not being petty, insensitive or heartless if you're newly divorced and claim your pain level is a two or three, nor are you being weak, self-pitying or immature if you claim your pain level is at an eight or nine.

During the research of this book I interviewed several divorcees and have included their stories, although I have changed the names of the people within these pages to protect their privacy. You will find that each story is unique, and the levels of pain differ in each case; some divorcees say they experience a pain level of two or four. Others didn't hesitate to say they were experiencing a pain level of ten.

I'm sure that as you read these stories you will find that while each divorce was quite different from the others, all of them are similar in that the people going through them felt as though they were faced with burdens greater than those they would have faced had they lost their spouses through death.

The purpose of this book is to raise awareness among readers that many people are affected by divorce—whether by their own or that of another—and to help them understand that in many cases, losing a spouse through divorce can be as painful if not more so than losing him or her through death. It provides a variety of true stories to help readers relate, encouraging advice to let go of their feelings of guilt or shame while going through the healing process, and hope that there is life after divorce.

"Someday you're gonna look back on this moment of your life as such a sweet time of grieving. You'll see that you were in mourning and your heart was broken, but your life was changing." –Elizabeth Gilbert, Author

CHAPTER 1: GRIEF

"One of the hardest things you will ever have to do my dear is grieve the loss of a person who is still alive." –Jeannette Walls, Author

Earl and Bernice began dating when she was still in high school and they married shortly after her graduation. He was twenty-three and she was eighteen. They had four sons during the first twelve years of their marriage. During that period of time Earl had several occupations; one of those was as a part-time pastor at several local churches. Bernice held various part-time jobs as well, eventually settling into becoming a school bus driver and working for the local county sheriff's department.

They had their share of marital problems and discussions but there were no shouting matches or incidents of abuse. They just slowly began drifting away from each other, however, and it seemed that the further they drifted, the harder it became for them to rekindle their marriage. After twenty years of marriage, they decided to split and informed their children that mom and dad were divorcing. It would take about a year-and-a-half for the divorce to be complete. Their sons were twenty, nineteen, fourteen, and eight when the divorce became final.

The divorce was amicable. There were no custody battles, no debates about alimony, no fights over property. They agreed on a date when Earl would move out but decided that up until then he would continue to live with the family.

The eighteen-month period leading up to the divorce was a

very sad time for their eldest son—that was me, Stanley.

While dad was still at home, he and I carpooled together back and forth to work. We both worked for a factory that had two locations about a mile apart from each other. My dad worked in the part that produced car tires and I worked at the other producing floor tile. He tolerated my taste in music during those car rides…at the time I liked southern rock, especially Lynyrd Skynrd…and we would chat about work and the weather and other everyday things. But we never spoke about the pending separation and divorce.

I will never forget the last day that we carpooled to work before he moved out of the house. As I was driving us back home, I realized that this would be the last time I would ever carpool with my dad. It was a surreal moment. I felt as if someone close to me was dying, as if I had just lost my dad. Instead of the death of a loved one, it was the death of my dreams, hopes, goals and expectations for my life that would never come to fruition.

Comanche

What is grief? It is defined as "keen mental suffering or distress over affliction or loss" which covers traumatic experiences such as death and divorce. Everyone has experienced suffering and distress such as a loss of a job, death of a family pet, leaving friends or family to move to a new town—the list goes on. According to Kenneth C. Hauck in his book, *A Time to Grieve,* people grieve due to the loss of something or someone they value. There is no monopoly on grief. Everyone will experience grief of some type at some point in their lives.

I remember as a young boy grieving over the loss of my pet dog Comanche because she was my companion and best friend, always by my side when we took long walks in the woods. What breed was Comanche? She was what people would call a mutt, she wasn't small but not big, she was in between and had a mixture of short brown and black fur. She was very heroic. I remember one time when we were walking in the woods behind our house when we encountered a pack of wild dogs. I remember Comanche placing herself between the pack and my brother and me to protect us from the other dogs. I was scared but having Comanche for protection helped assuage my fears. The other dogs eventually left the area and we continued our walk and play time in the woods with our protector.

The death of Comanche was very traumatic. We lived in the rural part of our state of Alabama. There were wide open spaces and very few cars on the road, so Comanche wasn't confined to the house and was free to roam about the yard. One day she apparently wandered too close to the rural, country road and was struck by a car and killed. I remember kneeling by her side crying. I felt so stupid because she was a pet and not a human being. *Why should I grieve for a pet?* I realized later in life that Comanche was a valuable part of my life and her loss caused me to grieve, which was not stupid after all.

But the death of Comanche would not be my most traumatic experience. My parents' divorce has been the one event in my life that has caused me to experience the most grief. The death of both of my parents later in life would cause me some mourning, but it was nothing compared to the pain I felt with their divorce. Death was easier to accept because everyone dies—but not everyone gets divorced—especially not *my* parents.

Death of a Dream

There is a difference between experiencing grief based on the death of a loved one and that which involves a divorce or death of a dream.

Someone who loses his or her spouse through death is expected to grieve, and well-meaning family and friends will tell the surviving family members to take time to heal and go through the grieving process. There is a funeral and a designated time and place to find some closure with the death of a loved one. It's very normal and expected for someone to grieve over someone dying.

There is a natural tendency to express condolences when someone shares the news that a family member or friend has passed. Nearly everyone has experienced the death of a loved one and the absence of that person usually will cause great grief.

There are usually numerous memories shared during the mourning and grieving process of how the deceased person affected the lives of countless others. Many comfort themselves with happy memories of the past as they look through photos or watch video slide shows that replay scenes of the loved one interacting with family and friends at birthday parties, social events or community gatherings.

People may carry those pictures around with them for days and weeks after the death of a loved one, recounting the great times that they had with each other. During this time there is normally nothing but praise and admiration heaped upon the deceased. And most importantly, there will be an empty chair at the dining room table at family dinners where the deceased used to sit, at least for a time, to remind family members of their loss.

Divorce is different. Many divorcing couples, as well as their friends and family members, will go through stages of grief; however, there isn't a grieving process nor an appointed date and time to share their grief with loved ones such as a funeral where people come together to help find closure.

During the days leading up to the divorce there may be one or even a few close confidantes to comfort the couple as the marriage crumbles. But the day the divorce is finalized is usually the opposite of the day a person dies—the divorcing partners spend it alone, not surrounded by family and friends. There is no group of people to help provide closure that day, or even in the days to come—no ceremony, no photos, no sharing of memories…no expression or sharing of grief over the loss. Nothing.

It can be difficult to know what to say to someone who has experienced a loss. The safe thing to say at funerals is "condolences" or "sorry for your loss." But how are people supposed to respond when they hear that a family member or friend has recently divorced? Do they say, "I'm happy for you, best thing that could have happened to you," or "I'm sorry for your loss?" Of course it depends on the nature of the divorce and who initiated it. One partner might be glad it's over while the other partner has just had his or her world turned upside down and is deeply grieving.

Many times the divorcing partners and their children will have questions or concerns about how to act or what to say or even how they should feel going forward. What can be tough is when divorced partners or children from the marriage feel like their world has just caved in and they are in mourning, while a friend who has recently divorced is not sad but is happy or even ecstatic. Someone going through the divorce or affected by it may ask, "What is wrong with me? Am I weak? Am I supposed to grieve? Am I supposed to be happy?" Many will put up a stoic front pretending everything is ok because friends and family members are actually congratulating them. What they may really want to hear is "sorry for your loss" because the divorce has caused and is continuing to cause grief.

For me the days leading up to and the finalization of my parents' divorce was a difficult time for me. The thought of my parents not living together was something that was hard to comprehend. All of my life I was accustomed to coming home and having both parents around the house. Also I was the eldest and I felt that I had to shoulder the responsibilities of the "man of the house" and step up and be a leader for my three younger brothers. However, the last thing I wanted was the responsibility of a household; if I had wanted that I would have gotten married.

And finally, and most devastating for me, our family had struggled financially most of our lives and our financial situation had recently just turned positive. We had always rented before and had just recently moved into a home that we owned. We still had financial struggles but we finally had achieved the "American dream"...owning our own house. It really wasn't a new house, it was a mobile home and was actually not new but used; still it was an awesome accomplishment for our family, having our very own home.

The "American dream" was short lived for me though when twelve months later my dad loaded his clothes into his car and drove away. Mom, my brothers, and I still lived in the trailer, but my dream of having a complete family was gone.

I tried to look at the situation as a "glass half-full." I told myself it wasn't like one of my parents had died, so it shouldn't have been a big deal, yet I was grieving. I realized couples get divorced every day and kids still get to see their parents. But to me it wasn't about seeing my parents—it was about the death of a dream of having a family made up kids and a mom *and* dad.

When I was grieving and sad, I felt like I was a wimp and I needed to toughen up and display a "stiff upper lip" and act like a man. *Why should I be sad when both of my parents were still living and I could still see both of them?* Yet I felt like someone or something inside me had died and I felt all alone in trying to handle it, wishing I had someone who understood, someone to talk to about all I was feeling and experiencing. I'm sure now looking back that I would not have felt so self-doubting, isolated and alone as a teenager had one of my parents died.

Waiting for the Storm

There is a story that can be found on the internet about two people standing on a beach: One is facing toward the storm and the other one is facing away from it to show how someone may experience grief based on whether a loss (be it through death or divorce) was expected or unexpected.

There are those whose experience is similar to someone standing on the beach facing the water who can see the storm forming and slowly advancing toward them—they can prepare for the impact. In these cases, there is time to mentally and emotionally prepare for the final day. When a loved one is diagnosed with a terminal illness, death is usually imminent and friends and family members can prepare for it. When this is the case, the person dying will usually receive hospice care which indicates the final phase of the terminal illness.

Likewise, a couple may be in a marriage that has been "terminal" for years and it is just a matter of time before it is expected to die. In this instance, the "death" of a family through divorce can be very similar to experiencing a death through terminal illness. In many cases a marriage has been "dying" for years, but both partners stay married due to financial benefits or for the kids. Each partner will nurse the marriage and attempt to keep it on life support as long as possible but eventually, despite all of their efforts, the couple decides to "pull the plug" and their marriage succumbs to death.

Even in the case where you can see the storm coming, even when you're prepared and you can see the end is near, divorce is worse than death. When a loved one is diagnosed with a terminal illness and the family is told he or she only has months or a year to live, they will rally around the dying person and band together to provide care and comfort. During the months leading up to the death there will be moments where many family members may begin the grieving process together before their loved one dies. When death comes there can even be a feeling of relief that the person has passed on "to a better place."

There is usually no such shared comfort or effort to rally around a "dying" marriage and, even if it is expected, the end can be emotionally draining and sometimes downright depressing. Just like death, there are months leading up to the divorce when the partners know it is just a matter of time until their marriage succumbs to divorce. There may be relief when it is finally over but there may also be pain, guilt, and grief.

I was not blindsided by my parents' divorce and could see it coming. I had time to grieve and prepare for the end. Still, while I could steel myself for the impact of the wave coming my way, I still had to feel it crash, cold and hard, upon me. I still felt fear as I watched it looming and soaked in grief after that wave washed over me. It felt like I was watching a wave crash into a sandcastle that I had spent all my life building on a sandy beach, and then slowly recede leaving nothing but a remnant in ruins.

During the divorce process, which lasted for eighteen months, I experienced grief during the end stage of the marriage and after the divorce. As the end approached I began feeling more and more grief and it was not about losing one of my parents but the grief of losing my life as I knew it—the death of my happiness, my childhood, my dreams.

Like many children, I had hopes and dreams of my family staying together, with my mom, dad, and three brothers, the way God had intended it to be. On the day the divorce became final, there was no celebration of life, just a feeling of loneliness. I did feel relief that the "sickness" was over, but I also felt a void. There was always the empty chair my dad had formerly occupied during family dinners to serve as a reminder. I grieved too for my dad because he was moving out of the house and worried about what would happen to him and whether he could make it on his own.

Then there are those who are truly blindsided by a death or divorce. Their loss is depicted by someone who is facing away from the ocean and is completely unaware that a storm is brewing and has no time to brace for the impact. The huge waves crash and the first reaction is one of stun and shock. The grief process can take longer and can be more complicated in those who have lost someone unexpectedly or have been blindsided by a partner requesting a divorce; they receive no warning, no time to prepare mentally or emotionally, so when the wave hits them, they are truly brought to their knees.

For those whose partners want a divorce when they do not, the impact can be especially hard. And for those who unexpectedly find out that their partners are having an affair or choose to leave them for another, the tidal wave can knock them to the ground with such force that it can be devastating in its destruction.

Tracy lived down the road from Brian's family and knew his mom and dad but had never met him until he started dating Tracy's friend Lucy. One day while Brian and Tracy were chatting, he told her that he and Lucy were finished and he would like to spend time with her. She was fourteen and he was seventeen when they began hanging out and occasionally dating. When she turned eighteen, Tracy and Brian began having a serious relationship and dated off and on for the next seven-and-a-half years until he finally asked her to marry him. The couple decided to have a small wedding at the courthouse with a judge and a few witnesses.

During their time together they had five kids—four daughters and one son. Brian worked as a home contractor and Tracy worked at home for the first year of the marriage before landing a job working at a hospital. Everything was going well for the family until three-and-a-half years into the marriage. Brian was devastated when both of his parents passed away at the same time. After that his attitude toward Tracy turned domineering and possessive and he didn't want her working outside the home. When she told him she wanted to attend a girls' evening out after work, he became upset and jealous so she didn't go, nor get together with friends after that, but continued to work her job despite his protests.

Tracy experienced the shock of her life when she found that her husband was seeing another woman. She confronted him with an ultimatum to choose between her and his mistress. To her shock Brian chose the mistress, leaving her to wonder why her husband would choose another woman over his wife and the mother of his children. When he left, she couldn't eat or sleep, and she would beg him to come back every time he visited the kids. He was her best friend and it would hurt her deeply when her friends would try and console her by telling her that her husband leaving was the "best thing that could have happened" to her. That's not what she wanted to hear. To her, Brian leaving was not the best thing but the worst thing that could ever happen. Her heart was broken.

Tracy and Brian had seemed like the "All-American" couple, living in a beautiful home in a modest neighborhood with five beautiful children. They were both working good jobs and each had excelled in their careers. They were truly like a royal family living in Camelot.

Then the walls of Camelot began falling apart. Tracy had thought her marriage was going great and then without warning she was blindsided by the tsunami that crashed over her when Brian wanted a divorce.

Stages of Grief

Grief is experienced by everyone. Depending on the book or blog you read about it, there are various opinions on the stages of grief someone experiences when going through the process. Most authors on the subject use stages of grief to identify the varying emotions experienced when dealing with a loss. The number of stages of grief can vary from five to up to ten depending on these emotions.

The Kübler-Ross model first introduced by Swiss-American psychiatrist Elisabeth Kübler-Ross in her 1969 book, *On Death and Dying,* described five stages of grief. L.J. Burke introduced seven stages of grief in his *Seven Stages of Grief During and After Divorce* article published in *Divorce Magazine.* In his book *Good Grief,* Granger E. Westberg described ten different stages for grief that a person experiences when some trauma occurs in his or her life.

I chose the Kübler-Ross five-stage model because, in reflecting back on my parents' divorce, it was easier for me to identify with the five stages when dealing with my own grief. At the time I experienced all five phases: denial, anger, bargaining, depression, and acceptance.

Each person will experience different phases in varying order, and some phases will be revisited. I wish I had known about the phases when my parents were going through the divorce. Maybe it would have helped me realize that grief is a process that shouldn't be hidden or denied and that it's not something about which I should have felt embarrassed or ashamed.

Denial

Denial is the phase where you don't want to deal with something that is happening in your life—kind of like an ostrich putting its head in the sand to hide from the attacking lion, there is a mindset of "what you can't see can't hurt you." Some people seem to believe or feel that not dealing with death or divorce will help keep the pain away; if you don't think about it maybe the people involved will change their minds and in some strange way a miracle will occur and save the day.

Denial was the first phase that I really went through because I remember the months leading up to my parent's divorce and how I didn't really want to think about it or talk about it. I didn't even talk to my friends and tell them what was happening in my family. My friends and I would go out for the evening and party but I never confided in any of them about my parents' pending divorce. For some reason not dealing with it kept the pain at bay and meant I could hide the shame I felt that my parents were getting divorced. I thought if any family should stay together it would be ours.

Anger

Anger is the second phase and is an emotion that causes us to feel rage toward something that is hurtful. This is one stage that can continue to be revisited during the process. An event like a death or divorce can cause someone to feel anger toward a person or even God.

My parent's divorce was very painful and I experienced a lot of anger. I was angry because I was helpless that this event would change my life; no matter what I said or did, I couldn't stop the divorce. I didn't know which parent I should be angry with during the time because in my eyes, each could have made more of an effort to stop the divorce process. Then there was God. *Why couldn't the Creator of the universe, Creator of man save my parents' marriage? Save my family?!*

Bargaining

Bargaining is when we attempt to negotiate an outcome that favors our desires. We may find ourselves trying to make a deal with God to save a marriage in exchange for an action or sacrifice on our parts. You may negotiate with your spouse and start thinking that things are not as bad as they seem and find yourself giving more and hoping that your spouse will reciprocate.

I didn't know how to or what to bargain for with my parents because what was happening to me was out of my control. There was one night though that clearly sticks out in my memory. I drove my dad's pickup to a secluded cemetery. While I sat alone in my dad's truck drinking vodka, I remember thinking about bargaining...*but how could I bargain when the situation was totally out of my control?* There's no bargaining with parents if they have already made up their minds to go through with the divorce. I didn't see any sense in bargaining with God. *What did I have that God needed?* He already had my soul. I felt hopeless. I looked at the vodka bottle. *Maybe if I stopped drinking, God would save my parent's marriage?* But then I realized that would just be a fantasy, and I chugged a few more swallows.

Depression

Depression is the fourth stage and as discussed here is not considered "clinical depression" which is a medical disorder (and anyone suffering from clinical depression should seek medical attention). Depression discussed here is a mood disorder causing sadness or a feeling of loneliness.

Depression was the worst stage for me and I spent a lot of time dwelling in it. I had a continual feeling of sadness even when people around me were having fun. I remember going to a party and there was dancing and laughter and everyone was socializing. I remember faking a smile that should have won an Academy Award for acting—pretending I was having a good time. But down deep it was hard for me to relax much less have fun because I was preoccupied with my crumbling family situation. It's a strange feeling to be at an event where you know you should be happy and enjoying yourself but you can't muster the energy. Even though I was surrounded by people I felt alone.

It was hard to feel happiness when my world was ending, at least the world that I had known. I guess for me the divorce of my parents was the death of my dream that we would be a family and it left a hole that no amount of vodka or fun could fill.

Acceptance

Acceptance is the fifth phase when you admit and embrace the situation as it is actually happening. Entering this stage doesn't necessarily mean that you are at the end of your grief process. Oftentimes accepting the fact that the divorce is happening causes one to go back to the anger stage or the depression stage.

I remember the night when I finally accepted the fact that my parents were divorcing. I had gotten off from work, showered, and decided to meet up with some friends at Larry's house so we could catch up with each other. When I arrived at his house, there were a couple of friends already there. I remember standing outside smoking a cigarette, leaning up against my car, and we were talking about what we were going to do that evening.

That's when Larry looked at me and said, "My mom heard that your parents are getting a divorce and wanted to know if it was true. I told her that you hadn't mentioned anything, but I would ask you."

That's when after months of hiding the fact from friends, I had to confess, "Yes it's true. My parents are getting divorced."

He responded, "What a bummer. Sorry to hear that. Let's go and drink some "tater juice" (vodka)." That was the evening that I was forced to accept the fact that my parents were breaking up and that the divorce was inevitable.

Conclusion

Death and divorce will both bring grief, but the word itself and the typical grieving process will be associated more often with death than divorce.

With the death of a loved one, people are quick to send you sympathy cards, to pray for you and to expect you to take time to grieve. There are some folks who will send a follow-up sympathy card a few weeks later because they recognize the pain you are experiencing can last quite a while.

With divorce there are no sympathy cards, no prayers, no "time off" to grieve. In fact, you can't even find a divorce sympathy card on the shelves of your favorite greeting cards store.

The wife of a colleague died recently and when I saw him, I naturally said, "Sorry for your loss." My colleague responded, "Thank you." Providing condolences when someone loses a loved one through death seems to be the respectful and expected action. But what do I say to someone who tells me that he or she was recently divorced? "Sorry for your loss," or "Let's go celebrate?" What do you say? Whether the results will be good or bad for one or both members of the divorcing couple, there is still grief involved because no matter what happened to bring it about, there is still the loss of a dream in the end.

In his blog, *Divorce and Grief,* Stephen Moeller discusses how grief and divorce are "rarely talked about in the same sentence." Couples have many reasons for ending a marriage—from infidelity to a mutual understanding of the need to go their separate ways. The unraveling marriage has most likely already brought plenty of grief so many believe that relief will come once it's over, ending the grieving process. But that's not always the case for all involved.

In reality both relief and grief can co-exist. Whether faced with divorce or death, the Moeller article states that "the challenge is to deal with those feelings of grief that are often a hidden part of the aftermath."

We all experience grief. It's ok to grieve for the death of a dream even though your feelings are hidden from the world. Only you know the reality of what you are feeling.

My parents' divorce has been the most traumatic and painful event in my life. The good part is that even while grieving and feeling sad, I could maintain my relationship with both parents. No, they had not died, and I was able to continue seeing and spending time with both parents, just not both at the same time.

And that pain caused me to write this book. At the time of this writing, both of my parents are deceased. Prior to their deaths I was able to spend time with each individually to discuss the reason that they divorced. I literally asked each of them, "Why did you get divorced?" Both responded that the cause of their divorce was pride. They started down the path of divorce and felt they couldn't turn back. Today when I think of both parents being dead I feel some sadness, but it is nothing like the sadness I still feel today when I reflect on their divorce. Still, today I do know ways to deal with my sadness as an adult that don't have to involve my old habits as a teenager of denying my feelings, being angry at my parents, bargaining with God, or trying to drink my way out of depression. I can feel my feelings or talk about them to a family member, friend or even God, remain in the acceptance phase of my grief, and be ok with that.

There's *"a time to weep and a time to laugh, a time to mourn and a time to dance."* Ecclesiastes 3:4 (NIV)

CHAPTER 2: CHILDREN

"Don't ever talk trash to a child about their other parent. After all, you found some good in them long enough to reproduce!" –Unknown

Laura was a very happy sixteen-year-old girl who was content with her life and, as an only child, enjoyed spending time with her mom and dad. She enjoyed high school and hanging with her friends and doing all the things that teenage girls do. She started noticing that her parents were having marital issues, but she didn't think much of it because in her mind all parents had them; they were just being "normal" and she wasn't concerned.

Then it happened, something that she never thought would occur in her life—her mom and dad were splitting up and even worse, her mom and she would have to move from her childhood home. Her dad had chosen to move in with his girlfriend leaving her and her mom with no other choice but to find other affordable living accommodations.

Her heart was broken. She loved her dad. Before the divorce, they would do activities together such as play basketball in the driveway. On weekends her dad and she would go hiking or spend time just hanging out together. She had a great fun-loving relationship with him.

But then it all changed for the worse.

Children are always a special concern when a parent dies or a family falls apart. Adults want to be able to protect children from dangers or bad events that may occur and strive to fill their childhoods with wonderful memories because most adults can relate to some bad experience in their own lives, whether it was the loss of a loved one or the death of a favorite pet. Even children want to help other children work through sad times.

Death and divorce are both sad events, but often a child feels like divorce is worse than death.

No Funeral to Say Goodbye

One of the first major differences between the death of a parent and the breakup of a family is that with death there is a formal process such as a funeral to say goodbye to a deceased parent. A funeral allows the family to come together and celebrate the life of a loved one which sets in motion a process for consoling a child whose life has changed forever.

Contrast that with divorce: there is no formal process in which a child is surrounded by friends and loved ones to say good-bye to a dream—a dream that was quashed because two adults made a decision that not only ended their own dreams, but those of the child.

The funeral is the formal process that allows a child to say good-bye to a deceased parent where family, friends, and co-workers come together to pay respects and say goodbye. This is a time that can bring comfort to the family that has lost a loved one. Family members come together to share stories filled with childhood memories of the deceased, where everyone usually reflects on the good times. Co-workers and friends of the deceased share stories of a mischievous childhood activity or significant work project providing the family with a positive view of the deceased parent.

Children learn fun, loving details about their parent that they never knew. There is usually no opportunity to contradict the stories and no one would think of making a derogatory statement about a parent that just died. Even though there is a formal process, the child will still experience pain and sorrow after the funeral and burial of a parent, but the formal process provides finality and leaves the child and family feeling like they were able to do one last special act for the deceased.

Unlike the day of a funeral, when the divorce is finalized there are not a multitude of family members surrounding and consoling the child. The only formal process usually involves the signing of the divorce papers. There is no funeral to allow closure nor a "celebration of life."

The informal process experienced by a child during divorce may involve the parents sharing the news that they are splitting up. In some cases, it may be left to one parent to tell the child about the divorce because the other decided to walk out, leaving him or her with the difficult task of consoling the child. This discussion may come after the marriage has slowly been crumbling for months or even years, or it may come abruptly without any warning.

In many cases during the divorce process, the parents continue to live together until the divorce is final and then the morning arrives when the child wakes up having to say goodbye because one parent is moving out. The kid may ask, "When will I see you again?" and the only truthful answer is that it depends on another formal divorce process called "custody."

With the breakup of Laura's family, she learned first-hand that there is no process where family and friends come together to share and cherish stories of happy memories. Instead Laura encountered a shattered family, and being an only child, she had no other siblings to confide in during the time leading up to and the finalization of the divorce.

Her father walking out of her life left her with feelings of betrayal and wondering how her dad could treat his only daughter this way since they had always been so close. In her mind, her dad had chosen to leave her and she had no idea when she would see him again, and she started to face the fact that she may never see him again even though he was still alive.

For her, there would at least have been finality and closure if he had died because, while he would be gone, she would be left with great memories, and it would not feel like he had chosen to walk out of her life. While she would still mourn that there would be no more summer basketball games or hikes, she wouldn't have to wonder about the future. If her father had only died she would have been left with happy memories of her dad playing basketball with her on those warm summer nights instead of anger and sadness that he had left her.

Custody

The second major difference between divorce and death is the word "custody."

Custody is a word that is normally reserved for cases of divorce where children are involved. Of course there is always the chance that custody may become an issue with a death of a parent, but this is rare, or at least we don't think of custody when we see a child standing beside the casket of a parent mourning.

In the case of divorce when children are involved, the word custody will come up during discussions because parents will need to work through the details as to whom will be the caregiver for the children even if the split is mutual. In some situations, custody discussions will be amicable in which each parent will agree to the care of the child and will make a decision that is best for him or her, thereby reducing stress. However, in many cases the resulting custody discussions may turn into battles where each parent will draw the line and fight for their own desired outcomes.

Parents need to always remember that kids will normally love both parents and will have developed their own unique bond with each parent that is different from the bond that the parents have developed with each other. Even though the parents may grow apart and may at times even develop a hateful relationship with each other, the child will still love both parents, and can be hurt to hear them degrade or bad mouth each other. Parents should remember that kids typically love both their father and mother no matter what, but too many times during the custody phase of the divorce a child may end up hearing derogatory statements directed toward one or both parents.

Then there are the custody cases in which one parent waives all rights to his or her children. In these cases, this might be the optimal decision so there isn't a dispute as to who will care for the children. The negative result in these situations is that children may feel that their estranged parent doesn't have a desire to spend time with them. In these custody cases the child may be left feeling abandoned and unloved.

Even though she didn't feel that way, Laura was fortunate that there was no stressful custody battle and her father waived his rights. If her dad had fought over custody, he would have made a bad situation worse. She was also lucky that her mother always attempted to speak well of her dad during and after the divorce.

Too many times though, custody disputes will turn into a battleground where the parents will hire lawyers who will fight on behalf of their client's desires. The disputes over custody often end up in court in front of a judge to determine the outcome. Each lawyer will argue on behalf of his or her client and a judge will have to weigh the facts in the case in an effort to make a fair decision.

A judge must weigh the options when the divorcing parents cannot agree on the best option for the child and each blames the other in an attempt to explain why the other parent is unfit to maintain custody. In some cases, the judge will have no other choice then to ask the child who is in the middle of the fight to take the stand to hear his or her side of the story. Many times, children are placed in an awkward position leaving them no other option then to answer questions in a way that may shed a negative light on one parent, allowing the other parent to take custody. In most situations the child loves both parents and doesn't want to say anything negative on behalf of either one but feels forced to do so.

When Joe was twelve, his mom and dad couldn't agree on custody arrangements which led to his parents hiring their own lawyers to fight for him. A court date was set for a judge to hear young Joe's custody case and he arrived in the court room escorted by his mom and her lawyer. Joe's dad sat with his lawyer waiting for the judge to call his case.

The time arrived for the judge to hear Joe's custody case. The two opposing lawyers attempted to debate and sway the judge to rule in their client's favor. Eventually Joe's mother's lawyer convinced his mom to allow Joe to take the stand in court to testify against his father, which would aid in his mother's efforts to gain full custody of Joe. This was a traumatic time for Joe because he cared for both parents but was forced to testify.

It has been twelve years since the divorce and Joe still remembers the day when he had to testify in court against his dad. He was always taught that when you testified in court and you placed your hand on the Bible, you had to tell the truth. You couldn't lie. He didn't want to answer the lawyer's questions, but he knew he couldn't lie and had to tell the truth about his dad. And because of that day in court he believes that his dad is still angry twelve years later. Joe still craves his dad's affection, he feels guilty, and he still thinks about what he could have done differently when he was twelve years old. He thought at the time that living with his mom would be best, but sometimes he feels like he chose to live with the wrong parent. Maybe if he had chosen his dad, they would have a better relationship now. But then again, he wonders, what type of relationship would he have had with his mom?

Custody Case Continues

There are the times, however, when the hard-fought custody battle is finally over and a judge has ruled, but the case still continues long into the future. In some cases the judge may have ruled for full custody for one parent or split custody between both parents. Both parents believe the battle is finally over but in some cases the custody dispute can continue for years based on changing circumstances that will require additional visits to court. The dispute may be over visitation where one parent wants to change the custody arrangements from the one agreed to at the beginning of the divorce. Of course in these situations the child will be caught in the middle again and cannot help but hear the parents discuss custody, which can fill him or her with guilt, grief, and remorse.

Tony has encountered many repeat visits to court during his bitter divorce and custody hearings which have continued for ten years since his divorce was finalized. Tony's feeling is that his ex-wife believes she can hurt him by limiting the time he spends with his children, which also provides her with an opportunity to build a better relationship with the children and tell them how bad a parent Tony is in hopes to have her kids become her allies in the divorce. The stress of the custody battles has weighed heavily on one of his sons to the point where he is undergoing intense therapy.

I had been interviewing Tony for my book and he and I had been talking for about an hour. I finished my last question and jotted down his answers bringing the interview to an end. I was getting ready to leave but Tony told me to wait—he had a book that he wanted to show me. When he returned, he handed me a copy of *Taken into Custody: The War Against Fathers, Marriage, and the Family*. He told me to take the book. He said he tried to read the book but every time he opened it he got physically sick to his stomach because he was reminded of his own custody battle for his daughter and two sons; at the time his daughter was eight and his sons were ten and six. The book discusses how the court system treats men unfairly when it comes to custody cases by unfairly awarding in favor of mothers instead of dads. Tony experienced this firsthand.

Tony lost the fight for fifty-fifty custody of his kids and the experience left him with deep mistrust for the court system. He still gets physically sick to his stomach when he is reminded of his custody case. In a court review of the children and the family, the results stated that both parents should have joint custody—but the judge's ruling was not for joint custody—instead it was for the wife or mother to have sole custody. The judge ignored the experts.

Tony eventually was able to get partial custody which allowed the kids to visit every other weekend and in the summer months every other week and then one week during

Christmas. If he had been a dad who had not been involved in his children's lives it would not have been bad, but he was one hundred percent engaged, so this was a very crushing compromise. He took some comfort in the fact that he was at least able to volunteer to coach and lead youth activities in which his kids participated, allowing him the opportunity to spend more time with his children.

Nine years have passed since the custody battle and while his sons do still come for visits and seem to have a good relationship with their dad, his daughter refuses to see him and doesn't really want to have much to do with him.

Tony believes that he was a victim of Parental Alienation Syndrome (PAS). PAS is when one parent "bad mouths," bashes, or verbally abuses his or her ex in front of the children, especially younger children that can be more susceptible to influence. The article, "What Is Parental Alienation Syndrome?" from Healthline 2019 states, "So PAS isn't really considered an official syndrome in the mental health or scientific fields, and it's not something your child can be diagnosed with. That doesn't mean the situation and its mental health effects don't happen." It may not be recognized as a syndrome, but parental alienation is still a big issue where one parent distances the children from their other parent. Some of the signs of this occurring is when a child has non-substantiated negative views or opinions of his or her other parent or grandparents. The children may be told that their other parent is to blame or is at fault for everything that has gone wrong in the marriage. The children will then grow up with a negative and incorrect view of their other parent.

Emy A. Cordano discusses some of the cultural beliefs about dads and moms in her blog "Why Do Women Get Child Custody In 90 Percent of All Cases? Isn't It Gender Discrimination?" In the blog she brings up culture as viewing moms as being better care givers to children. On the other hand, dads normally are in a better position to earn an adequate income to pay child support and alimony.

Denise encountered something very different than Tony

months after her divorce was over. She had initially been awarded custody of her two daughters, ages eleven and eight. Her ex-husband was content with this arrangement where he would visit his kids every Thursday and on the weekends. However, he eventually decided that he wanted more and took Denise back to court a year later to get partial custody of her daughters when they were twelve and nine.

She wanted to fight her husband, but her lawyer advised against fighting her ex for full custody. Her lawyer convinced Denise that it would be fair if her husband had the girls half the time. Denise took her lawyer's advice and she and her ex settled for fifty-fifty custody of the daughters. It may have been fair, but she wasn't happy; she wanted her kids all the time and she really began to despise her ex for taking her kids. She wanted to be with her children full time as she always had been and she was sad and resentful after that, feeling like she was missing half of her daughters' lives—and that she had given in and given up.

Today Denise often feels sad about not having the girls the other half of the time. Fortunately though, the arrangement didn't seem to negatively affect the girls. Ten years later, both daughters have a positive relationship with both parents and there isn't any resentment of either parent.

Remarriage/Blended Family

Death and divorce both bring opportunities for parents to remarry. In both situations a parent may marry again, and children find themselves becoming part of a new family consisting of a stepparent and possibly new brothers and sisters. This can be a time of fitting in and coping with new siblings and a new parent.

In the case of divorce, there may be a negative impact when a parent chooses to remarry and the new stepparent doesn't bond with the stepchild. In some situations, stepparents may not feel comfortable having a stepchild staying with them and will insist that the child live with the other parent. With death this is not even discussed. This can be an awkward situation leaving the child's parent to make a decision to select the child or to side with the new spouse. Too many times the child's parent will select the new spouse thinking that at least the child has the other parent that can care for him or her. This can cause a child to feel unloved.

This negative situation was experienced by two young sons, Johnny and Jimmy, when their dad remarried. Johnny was fifteen and Jimmy was eight, and shortly after their dad remarried, they wanted to spend time with their dad and live with him and his new wife. The new wife didn't want the sons staying with her and her new husband for any length of time because she had already raised her kids. This was a very important time in the lives of both boys where they needed to stay connected to their dad. This experience was very disappointing and disheartening for the young sons and left them feeling unloved and unwanted. This decision caused a rift between the boys and their dad and deeply damaged the relationship, which never healed.

The parent that the child is not living with may choose to remarry and in the process create a new family. Since the child doesn't live with this parent, this remarriage may cause the child to feel left out and unloved. Due to circumstances, this parent may spend most of the time with his or her new family leaving very little time for his or her own child. Children may become jealous when they see their mom or dad spending time with the new spouse's kids while neglecting them. These children often start wondering what is wrong with them and why their parent doesn't love them.

Leslie lived with her mom after her parents divorced. Her mom gained custody of her, but she was still able to have some weekends when she and her father spent time together. Leslie's dad eventually remarried a lady who had two daughters and she was welcomed to stay with the new family, but instead chose to continue to live with her mom.

As time went by Leslie saw her dad spending more time with her stepsisters because she was living with her mom. The time that she spent with her dad began decreasing and the time spent had to be shared with her stepsisters. Leslie began feeling resentful of her stepsisters because her dad was choosing to spend more time with his new family.

One day Leslie had enough, and she confronted her dad. Her mom was supposed to pick her up at 3:00 pm, but Leslie was already outside at 2:30 pm waiting for her mom. It was a hot, humid day and her dad noticed her outside waiting and told her she could wait inside the house where it was cool. She told her dad that she didn't feel welcome and would rather wait outside in the heat instead of waiting inside. She said that she didn't want to come back for a visit because it would just be a waste of time since he never did anything with her when she visited.

Finally her mom pulled up and Leslie left that afternoon feeling devastated; after that she only visited on holidays or special occasions. It would be three years before she and her father reconciled their relationship.

Holding Out Hope

A child of divorce experiences one scenario that a child who loses a parent through death never does: in many cases in which the child has fun memories of both parents, the child secretly holds out hope that his or her parents will one day be reunited in marriage, bringing the family together. After the divorce is final, children may also draw conclusions as to who is at fault for breaking up their happy home. The one incident that can occur that will finalize the breakup of the family is when one parent decides to remarry. When one parent does decide to remarry that will put a nail in the coffin of the possibility of the parents reuniting. Often the child can feel resentment against the parent that remarried, blaming that parent for killing the chances of ever being reunited again as a family.

Jason and Sally had been married several years and had three sons. They seemed to be a happy couple until Sally decided to leave her husband and sons for a better life. At the time the older son blamed his mom for the break-up of the marriage. Years passed and Jason began dating a young woman and eventually decided to marry. The son who had blamed his mom for the breakup of the family turned his blame on his father since his dad had killed any chances of reuniting the family, believing that his dad had broken the family up for good.

Shame or Embarrassment

In most cases the death of a parent doesn't cause a child to have feelings of shame because his or her parent died. Instead, children will experience compassion and love during the time of their loss.

A child who is going through the separation or breakup of their parents' marriage, however, will often feel some portion of shame. Children tend to not discuss the breakup of their parents' marriage because of what their peers will think of them. School age kids are susceptible and vulnerable to this perceived negative image while in school. These feelings of self-consciousness, low self-esteem and shame are real, whether they are justified or not. Kids want to be able to portray that everything is ok with their parent's marriage and keep hoping that the marriage will heal and they won't have to tell anyone.

Laura was embarrassed that her family was breaking up because her parents were divorcing, and she worried about what kids at school would say or think. She no longer felt comfortable going to the high school that she had once loved. Once her parents divorced, she decided she wanted to drop out of high school altogether. Her mom convinced her not to quit school and instead worked to find a different high school that Laura could attend. Laura decided to change schools and to begin attending classes at a new school where no one would know her past. The new school made Laura feel as if she had a fresh start.

Conclusion

When a child loses a parent through death there is a formal process with some closure; with divorce that usually doesn't happen. With death the child is comforted by people sharing wonderful memories about the deceased parent; with divorce people may share less than flattering comments about one or both parents. With divorce the child holds out hope for reunification of their parents and family, which is something a child of a deceased parent will never have. But these hopes, often dashed, often lead to more despair. Also with divorce, children may find themselves in the middle of a custody battle forced to choose one parent over the other. Finally, the divorced parent may choose to remarry causing a situation in which the child feels like he or she is no longer loved, or children of divorce may find themselves in a larger blended family where they feel left out. These are just a few comparisons and there are many more cases where divorce can indeed be worse than death.

Still, there can be some positive results that come with a family breakup through divorce. First, the child will normally still have access to, and a relationship with, both parents. A child may get a second chance to rekindle and even improve his or her relationship with the estranged parent. Parents who become divorced may realize that they have not been great parents, affording them and their children a second chance at having a better relationship.

Laura's story has a happy ending. Five years after her mom and dad divorced, they remarried, reuniting Laura's family. Laura and her dad were able to rekindle their relationship after several years apart. He realized that he had deeply hurt his daughter. There are no more summer basketball games at her childhood home, but they are now building other memories and having new adventures.

There is also a second chance when two divorced parents marry bringing children from their previous marriages together creating a blended family. While there are plenty of struggles and challenges, the end result can be beautiful and happy.

That is what happened to Marie when she remarried a man named Paul who had a son and daughter from a previous marriage. Marie also brought two children to the marriage, a son and daughter. There is always a concern that the siblings and stepsiblings won't get along with each other and/or with their stepparent. But if the parents of the new blended family remain positive and work hard at it, they can build a blended family that bonds and helps and supports one another.

Marie and Paul eventually discovered that blended families bring chances at new healthy relationships. Marie's daughter who was living at home with her and her new stepdad Paul soon bonded with her new stepbrother, forming a great relationship that neither had before with their own siblings.

"Sometimes when we least expect it, love gives us a second chance." —Jacqueline Simon Gunn, Author

CHAPTER 3: HOME

"Fight the tears back with a smile
Stop and look for a little while
Oh, it's plain to see
The only thing missing is me..."
(from the song, "Who's That Man?" –Toby Keith, 1994)

Chris remembers when he and his wife Melinda went shopping for their first home; at times the experience almost felt the same as trying to find someone to marry. There were many houses that appealed to them and would accommodate their needs but none of the homes had that emotional effect on him or his wife—that said, "this is the one."

They kept looking and after months of searching, they finally found the ONE—a home that spoke to them both emotionally, tugging at their hearts. Of course, once they found the house, they had to submit an offer to purchase it and then anxiously wait for the seller to accept their proposal. The seller accepted but the deal wasn't done yet because they had to apply for a loan. They were fortunately able to get the loan and using their life savings as a down payment, were able to purchase the home. It was the biggest investment they would ever make in their lives.

Chris and Melinda set out to turn the house into a place where they felt at home and where they were able to happily raise their two children. Chris planted a beautiful cherry tree in the front yard along with some tulips and daffodils that sprouted each spring and constructed a split rail fence on their half-acre property which allowed their German Shepherd puppy to roam. Inside, he spent many weekends painting each of the rooms of the home in the colors Melinda painstakingly picked out to make the house feel like it was theirs. With the help of some of his buddies, Chris also added hardwood flooring in the foyer, hallway and kitchen which added warmth and charm.

Chris and Melinda celebrated many birthdays, Christmas and Easter holidays, and hundreds of small but special family moments during the course of their eleven years of marriage.

Then the day came when Melinda filed for divorce and gave Chris thirty days to vacate the house. Chris lost his home which he had invested not only his life savings into, but his life.

There is a difference between selling the family home when a death occurs versus losing your home through divorce, and the emotions that are experienced with each.

Losing or selling the family home is "similar to losing someone you have loved in your life" according to Bruce Nemovitz in his article, "Selling Your Home: The 5 Stages of Loss and Grief," from the Laureate Group website (2019). Emotions run strong and powerful when it comes to the sale or loss of a marital or family home...but they can vary if the home is sold or lost through a death versus a divorce.

What Makes a House a Home?

"The house was trivial, just a material possession, a thing. What mattered was the home, my kids and the wife that I used to be married to." (Chris Dawson, fictional name of real man interviewed)

It is important to distinguish between a house and a home. A house is merely a building, a possession, a thing. A home is much more than brick and mortar; it is built with family, friends, good times, memories, a backyard with a favorite climbing tree, pets, neighbors and love.

When a couple purchases a house they will typically transform it into "their" family home by adding special touches such as paint, furniture, artwork and even architectural work to the inside, usually making outside improvements as well; perhaps they'll plant a garden, trees, shrubs, plants and flowers, maybe build a deck or patio or even add a hot tub, pool or playground equipment, and possibly surround the backyard with a fence so children and pets can play safely.

The couple designs their home from the inside out to match their tastes. The home will have mementos displayed throughout such as wedding china selected by the bride, that special painting the couple picked out together on that getaway weekend or the "interesting" vase that was a gift from Aunt Madeline. The home is where the family retreats when life is rough. It is for comfort, solace, and a relaxing evening after a hard day's work—their refuge and safety zone.

Social status and a perceived lifestyle are also important and play a role in the decision a couple makes in choosing which house to purchase. They may ask themselves, *what does this home say about me?* The ideal family home in a coveted neighborhood with a play area for the children located in a great school district can echo success, achieving the American dream.

Who Should Keep the Home?

Of all the assets that a couple will possess, the home is not just the largest financial asset but usually the most important and valuable.

With the death of a spouse, the surviving partner will not be asked, "Who gets the home?" The expectation is that the surviving spouse is expected to continue to live in the family home. No one would think about asking that question. As a matter of fact, legal advisors usually tell surviving spouses not to make any drastic decisions like selling the family home because of the emotional state in which they find themselves after the death of their loved ones.

However, with divorce the question, "Who gets to keep the house?" is usually the first one on everyone's mind. That is not an easy question to answer and may not be easily resolved.

The couple may be able to work out differences and decide

among themselves who should keep the home—or not.

There is the thought that "who keeps the house, keeps the kids," or at least has a better shot at it, which may seem unfair to some; but data shows when it comes to child custody, judges often rule in the favor of the spouse who keeps the house. If one of the parents is able to continue to live in the family home, then based on custody arrangements the children can usually continue to live there without much disruption. The children will still have their play area with which they are familiar and will still be surrounded by their friends.

Should the partners be left with no choice but to sell the family home, the quality of life for their children may suffer. With the sale of the home the children may have to move to a smaller house or apartment where they no longer have their play area or their friends. They may only have moved a few miles from their old home, but the move can "trigger feelings of insecurity, isolation, or anger, which are often seen in depression," according to the article, "How Moving Can Trigger Depression in Children," found on the Verywell Mind website, which urges divorcing couples to be mindful of their children being able to stay in the family home whether they split their custody and visitation times or not, and to try to keep to their children's routines at all costs.

Can I Afford to Keep the Home?

This question will arise whether there is a death in the family or death of a dream.

With the death of a spouse or a loved one the surviving family members will normally not worry about losing the family home. Most of the time when someone loses a spouse through death there is an insurance policy that can help offset the mortgage or, depending how long the couple has lived in the home, will pay it off. Surviving spouses are typically able to continue to live in the home until they pass away or make a decision to sell it. Of course, there is always a chance the surviving spouse didn't receive benefits to assist with the mortgage and will have to sell the family home to cover outstanding debts or in some cases will have to declare bankruptcy. But this is a rare occurrence.

Divorce is a situation in which both spouses will be asking themselves if they can afford to keep the family home or will it need to be sold, since the monthly mortgage payments may require the salary of both partners. Divorcing spouses may find themselves being forced into a position to sell their dream home because their partners quit the marriage. They feel that they are being robbed of the chance to keep their own home and may try to fight it although they realize they can't in the end. When neither partner can afford the monthly payments, the only option is to sell. The social status of the parents and children may change overnight as they downsize to a smaller home, apartment, or maybe even to their childhood bedroom in the house in which they grew up, sometimes with their own kids in tow.

There is always the option of one spouse "buying out" the other's financial interest in the family home. If the partners can agree to an equitable split, then one will be given the opportunity to find the funds to buy out his or her partner. Refinancing the existing mortgage will normally not decrease the monthly house payments significantly enough to make them affordable for the remaining single partner. A viable option that some partners choose is to reach out to family members, most likely their parents, for a loan to buy out their soon-to-be ex-partner, but it often still feels as if they are losing. Not only did they lose a spouse but then had to reimburse him or her to keep from losing the family home too. This can feel like blackmail. Still, if children are involved it may feel like it is the best or only choice.

Selling the Home

Selling the family home can be an emotional time for anyone, regardless of the reason behind it. Emotions will vary depending on three options that are presented to people who are facing this issue: they have a choice to sell, they have no choice *but* to sell, or they have no choice to sell—they will lose the home, *period*.

The first option usually has the most positive outcome. When people choose to sell the family home, they often use the proceeds to purchase their next dream home—a house that better fits their needs usually in a better neighborhood. The family will still experience sadness from all of the good memories made in the house they're selling, but they will take comfort knowing they will experience the joys of new memories they will make in the dream home.

The second option, when a family feels they have no choice *but* to sell their home (they don't want to do it but it's the best or right thing to do, whatever the reason may be), can result in negative emotions or grief. The article "Selling Your Home: The 5 Stages of Loss and Grief" discusses the grief that elderly people feel when having to sell the family home they have lived in for decades so they can downsize to a retirement community. There isn't much of a choice because they are no longer able to care for the home. In another situation illustrating this concept in the article, parents pass away and their surviving children reluctantly sell the family home, which is full of decades of great childhood memories. It's a bittersweet moment, but the right thing to do.

An article on The Mortgage Calculators website, "Talking to Your Kids About Losing Your Home: 4 Mistakes to Avoid," states that "It's hard enough…to move to a new house—but it is nearly unbearable when the choice to leave is not yours."

The third option can be the most emotionally traumatic of all—losing the home altogether without profiting from a sale, usually through foreclosure.

Foreclosure/Bankruptcy

A couple may find themselves in a position where they no longer have enough funds to pay the monthly mortgage payments. They may default on their loan in which case the bank takes possession of the home. There is sometimes an option available to avoid foreclosure such as a "short sale" in which the lender allows the homeowner to sell the house for a loss, or the bank agrees to buy the house and draws up a new deed in lieu of foreclosure. In all of these cases there is no profit and the family will be homeless.

From her article "Foreclosure & Divorce" found on the Nolo website, Amy Loftsgordon states, "divorce and foreclosure often go hand in hand." A couple faced with a bitter divorce may actually choose to let the house go into foreclosure. For whatever reason, whether they can no longer afford the payments or don't want to make them, one or both spouses may choose not to sell, letting the home go into foreclosure. Sometimes a spouse responsible for the mortgage chooses not to make the payments out of spite or out of a belief that it is unfair that he or she should have to bear the sole financial weight of paying the bank. The house may be left sitting vacant and rotting until the foreclosure is completed.

In some cases the couple agrees to sell the home but one is reluctant to do so and lets the house go into disrepair, decreasing its value, or delays the sale until a time when the market isn't favorable. The couple may break even or sometimes lose money on the sale because the current market price may have decreased or at least not increased and there is little equity in the home. By the time expenses from the sale such as realtor fees are deducted, there is little to no money left over.

In any of these cases, the homeowner(s) may feel they have been "robbed" of a choice to sell their home for a profit. This can cause all of the stages of grief to become exacerbated...and the feelings of denial, anger and depression, not to mention bargaining, that go along with it to become all-consuming.

Chris felt like he was robbed when he was ordered to vacate "his" home because of a court order made at the request of his soon to be ex-wife, Melinda. He pleaded with her to let him stay until he could find a place of his own, but his requests fell on deaf ears—she wouldn't change her mind.

Melinda seemed to be more interested in hurting him. Four weeks after vacating the house he decided to drive by one evening and felt traumatized by what he saw. He was heartbroken when he saw the overgrown lawn and weeds growing where flowers used to be since he was no longer there to care for the landscaping. But what really enraged him was when he discovered that Melinda's boyfriend was sitting at the patio table having dinner with his ex and his two children!

Bankruptcy can result when a family loses their home because of financial hardships by defaulting on loans and then is usually faced with a foreclosure, or the bank seizing the house to later auction it off. The Merriam-Webster dictionary defines bankruptcy as "utter failure or impoverishment (to make poor)."

The family will need to relocate and is often given short notice to move and vacate the premises to find shelter. Oftentimes during these situations, families may become homeless. If kids are part of the equation, there will be questions that the children will most likely ask. Here are three questions from *Talking to Your Kids About Losing Your Home: 4 Mistakes to Avoid* from the Mortgage Calculators website that kids will ask: "Are we going to be homeless? Will I get to keep all of the stuff in my room? Why can't we live here anymore?" This is an emotionally draining and vexing time for the family.

While bankruptcy and foreclosure resulting in the loss of a home can happen through the death of a loved one, it is much more typical as the outcome of a divorce.

Divorce itself can be referred to as the bankruptcy, failure or impoverishment of marriage. Often it resembles a one-two punch—the first punch splits the family apart and then the second punch knocks the family out of their home. During divorce one of the spouses may feel as if he or she is being forced to sell because the partner wants to quit the marriage and therefore robs him or her of the choice to stay.

You No Longer Live Here!

One partner may be forced to vacate the family home while allowing his or her spouse and children to live in the home. The couple may have tried marriage counseling, but the marriage has been rocky for a while so when one spouse files for divorce it doesn't come as a shock for either partner. Still, what does come as a shock is when one spouse works with his or her lawyer to have a judge issue an order to have the other partner move out. This is very hurtful. Sure the marriage is over, but it takes time to find a place to live, plus it costs money to get into an apartment. The court order may give the partner a time frame of thirty days to vacate the home or the order may be more like an eviction to leave immediately.

Divorce also differs when one partner is forced to move out of the family home. This usually does not happen with death.

With divorce, one partner may have to evacuate his or her home overnight. There are situations that occur in which one spouse is forced to move out of his or her house without warning when the other spouse changes the locks overnight, locking him or her out. Many times the one that has been locked out of the house will require a police escort when visiting his or her own home to take pictures of it along with the furniture, decorations, appliances, books and all belongings so he or she will have evidence in court just in case the ex chooses to dispose of anything without his or her permission.

There are times when a judge can issue an order to have one partner vacate the premises, forcing him or her from the family home. The judge may issue an order to vacate immediately or may give a thirty-day window to move or find somewhere else to live.

Chris found himself in this latter situation. But the thirty days did not give him a chance to find an apartment much less come up with the cash for a deposit and first month's rent. He contacted a friend who had a vacant studio that he could live in until he found his own apartment. He was very thankful for his friend's generosity. If the friend had not been there for him, Chris would have been forced to move in with his parents. Still, years later it is difficult and emotional for him to drive by his old family home…it still has his ex-wife, his children, the dog and the tree he planted; it has everything but Chris.

Chris's social status changed virtually overnight. He went from owning a home in a coveted neighborhood to virtually becoming homeless. He was not able to find an apartment and had to depend on the charity of a good friend. In the end, he was never allowed to move back to the family home and felt like he had lost everything.

Household Treasures

With death you don't have to worry about dividing mementos or family heirlooms you own jointly with a deceased spouse. With divorce a person can often lose prized possessions that the separating couple has spent the life of their marriage acquiring. These possessions may seem trivial, but each little trinket can be filled with memories.

While Marie and her first husband Ray were married, they acquired many keepsake items that they had each handpicked and selected, both individually and as a couple. To start off the marriage Marie had selected the wedding china and silverware, a beautiful set of each that she had dreamed of as a little girl. When she and Ray divorced, the wedding china and silverware suffered the same fate as the marriage. They were separated with Ray taking possession of the coveted wedding china and Marie walking away with silverware. For Marie, the loss of the china is still painful today. Sure the china was just a thing, but in some ways the splitting of the china and silverware represented the splitting of the marriage.

Conclusion

> *"That's my house and that's my car*
> *That's my dog in my backyard*
> *There's the window to the room*
> *Where she lays her pretty head*
> *I planted that tree out by the fence*
> *Not long after we moved in*
> *There's my kids and that's my wife"*
> *Who's that man, runnin' my life?"*

The chorus to the song "Who's That Man?" written and

recorded by country music singer Toby Keith highlights the emotional impact that husbands or wives may feel when driving past what was once their happy family homes. Notice the lyrics may contain the word "house" but it's the ingredients such as the backyard, the dog, and her pretty head that makes the house a home. He is no longer deemed as essential, part of, or belonging to the family home.

The family home is more than a house or a thing—it contains the elements that make it a home: a spouse, kids, wedding china, a dog, a fenced backyard where the kids play. Divorce is not only the "bankruptcy" of marriage but in many situations can be the "bankruptcy" of the family causing the couple to lose their home and their refuge; the American dream suddenly turns into a nightmare.

Losing the home is really the final blow that makes a couple realize that their marriage is truly over. The filing of divorce papers delivers the first blow, but the knockout punch lands with the loss of the family home and spells defeat...and means the dream is finally dead.

"Drive away one more time
Lot of things going through my mind."
("Who's That Man?" –Keith, 1994)

When he was suffering through his divorce, a friend told Chris that in five years he wouldn't recognize his life in an attempt to give him positive feedback at the time.

Spring forward twelve years later...Chris meets and marries his soulmate, Julie. They find a beautiful house that they both fall in love with and decide to make it their forever home. Chris, with the help of his new partner, begins adding those personal touches on the inside to match their taste such as paint, carpet, and a new set of wedding china. They then turn their attention to the outside and add beautiful shrubbery, flowers, and plant grass seed in hopes to have a lush green lawn. They add a sunroom that overlooks the beautiful yard. In the evenings, he and his bride like to relax by sitting in the sunroom, pointing their chairs to the west, holding hands, and drinking their favorite cocktails.

The grass is finally greener on the other side. No longer homeless, Chris has found a new soul mate, a new best friend, a new wife, a new home and a new dream that came true—he is building memories with his new bride while they watch the green grass grow and he can now sing a new song:

"Point our rocking chairs towards the west
Plant our dreams where the peaceful river flows
Where the green grass grows"
("Where the Green Grass Grows" –Wiseman and Leary, performed by country music artist Tim McGraw, released in July, 1998 as the fifth single from McGraw's *Everywhere* album)

CHAPTER 4: FAMILY

"I never imagined that divorce would be part of my life history or my family's legacy. When people say that divorce can be more painful than death, I understand why. But like any great trial, God uses everything for good, if we allow Him to heal us." –Kristin Armstrong, ex-wife of Lance Armstrong (American professional road racing cyclist)

Jeff and his wife Veronica met during high school and dated a few years before getting married. They didn't have a formal church wedding and were content standing in front of a judge who performed a civil ceremony. Jeff and his wife spent years working together and raising a family with two beautiful children. They were living the American dream; both had decent paying jobs by American standards, and they had purchased a modest home in the suburbs.

They would usually spend the holidays with Veronica's family because Jeff's relatives lived in a different part of the country making it more difficult to visit on special occasions. During the years of the marriage Jeff built a positive relationship with his new family and was well liked by Veronica's parents and siblings, especially her dad.

After eighteen years, Jeff and Veronica decided to end their marriage. Jeff had begun dating a woman that he had been introduced to by a friend from work and was smitten with her. He asked Veronica for a divorce.

Veronica, on the other hand, wanted to make the marriage

work and was willing to forgive her husband, and even asked what she could change for Jeff to choose her over the other woman. Jeff responded that the only thing he wanted was to cut the ties on their marriage and live with the new love of his life.

Over her objections, Veronica was not chosen and was replaced by someone else.

Divorce or death is usually tough on those who have grown close to someone who has married into their family.

With the death of a family member, the family will usually come together to mourn the loss of a loved one. With death both the family of the deceased and that of the spouse still living will come together and offer support to the surviving husband or wife. Even in situations where negative situations may have occurred during the life of the deceased, the family members will still come together and provide support for each other. Good or bad, the expectation in society is for everyone to be respectful and helpful.

Divorce can come as a shock or a disappointment to family members because they often don't know how to deal with the death of a marriage. Family members on both sides of the marriage have typically formed a bond and relationship with the couple. In many cases each partner in the marriage has been treated like a son or a daughter, sister or brother, and some family members may choose to take sides during or after the divorce. Often there is a belief that family members of a divorced spouse need to be loyal and choose a side—they are usually unable to stay neutral.

Telling the Family

Telling the parents and siblings about the death of a spouse or the breakup of a marriage is a difficult task. The news can sometimes come as a shock to family members who aren't expecting the death or pending divorce. In some cases, the death or divorce may have been anticipated. For example, a loved one may have battled a terminal illness such as cancer for months or years before succumbing to the disease or a marriage may have been deteriorating before succumbing to divorce; still, the news usually comes as a surprise since many couples keep their troubles to themselves.

With the death of a spouse, whether by an unexpected and quick accident or from lingering long-term illness, the surviving husband or wife will immediately alert family members by making phone calls or otherwise notifying everyone. Upon hearing the news of the death, family members typically react with sadness and will reach out to the surviving spouse to provide immediate support. The surviving spouse will have every expectation that the family is not disappointed and is there to provide any support needed, and that he or she will be met with sympathy.

The death of a marriage is very different because when family members are told there can be an uncertainty of how they will react when they hear the news. The feelings can be mixed based on the circumstances of the divorce, for example, who initiated it or why the split occurred.

The spouse having to relay the news to his or her family will often question himself or herself. *What will my family think? Did I not try hard enough to save my marriage? Am I a failure because I couldn't keep my marriage together and instead chose to walk out instead of saving it? Will family members be able to see what I have done to try and save the marriage, or will they be disappointed?*

For Veronica the divorce was already a low point in her life. She dreaded telling her family the news because she didn't know how they would handle it. Veronica put off telling her family about the pending divorce as long as she could. She felt that her family would judge her and think less of her because they would believe the breakup was her fault, believing she had not worked hard enough and had given up on her marriage. Time was running out as the date of the divorce rapidly approached. She finally worked up the courage and decided to rip the bandage off the wound and tell her family. Bad news is like bad wine, it doesn't get better with age.

The divorce came as a shock to Veronica's family because she had never confided in them about the turmoil leading up to it. She was pleasantly surprised when her family didn't blame her for the breakup and instead was very supportive.

If Veronica had lost her spouse through death, she would not have had to experience any of these doubts and worries. She would have had no hesitation or concerns reaching out to her family because telling them of the death of her husband would have been expected. She would not have experienced any awkward confrontations with her mother having to share painful memories of her marriage in hopes to win her mom to her side. With death she would have expected her family to automatically rally behind her and provide support without having to give them reasons to come to her aid.

Betrayal

Emotions of shock, sadness, or disbelief will occur when a family learns of the death of a loved one. Sometimes betrayal can be felt by the surviving family members because the death of a loved one can make a person feel as if the deceased left him or her even though there was no choice, but this is usually rare.

In many situations during a marriage, however, family members have supported each spouse forming a bond. A divorce can also seem like a betrayal to some family members. Take, for example, the husband who was a shining star and role model for the rest of the wife's family. Family members who might have idolized the husband will be left in shock as to what happened in the marriage. They may wonder, *how could this person make a choice to leave us?*

When Veronica told her family about the divorce they were heartbroken because they really cared for Jeff and thought he was the greatest husband and father in the world. He was a great provider for his family and had ensured that they had a nice home and attended church services on Sundays. He was a role model for Veronica's younger siblings. After she told her family about the pending split she realized that Jeff had not only betrayed her, his wife, but he had betrayed her parents and siblings – her entire family.

Veronica learned that Jeff had chosen not to tell his family about the split, so she made the decision to tell his family on his behalf. It was just as difficult for Veronica to tell her husband's family about the breakup as it was her own since his family had always had a high opinion of him as well. His family had always been willing to assist and help Jeff with anything and enjoyed coming for visits even though they lived in another part of the country. Since she was the one who had to break the news to his family it was even harder when she explained about the girlfriend. His family was in total shock. This caused many of his family members to support Veronica and break off ties with Jeff. The feeling of many was that he had not only thrown away his wife and children but now he had thrown away his own family.

Family Gatherings/Holidays

Holidays and family gatherings can be difficult times when it comes to death and divorce. There are many wonderful memories shared during family gatherings, and gaps appear if someone no longer attends.

During the years of a marriage, a loving couple builds family traditions attending special family gatherings and holidays. When the family congregates, each partner will naturally have built loving relationships with members of their spouses' families. When the marriage breaks up, these traditions—such as attending special events and holidays and enjoying family time—will be shattered just like the marriage. Rarely will the ex-partners spend time with each other's families after the breakup.

Plans sometimes change for those who lose someone through death, but the surviving spouse and children will usually still be invited over to the deceased partner's family's house for holidays and visits. Surviving spouses may not feel as comfortable visiting their in-laws without the accompaniment of their partners, but they will still be welcomed.

Jeff realized with the breakup of his marriage to Veronica

that he not only divorced his wife but had indirectly divorced her family as well. The loss Veronica's family experienced, especially the special relationship Jeff had built with her dad during the marriage, was not expected. It wasn't until the first holiday after the divorce that Jeff realized what he had lost. The first Christmas apart was especially painful. He eventually rebounded but it took time for Jeff to work through the breakup of not only his marriage but the loss of his ex-wife's family.

Veronica will never forget when she attended her first holiday event with her family after splitting with Jeff. Even though Veronica still had her family, she felt a void when she attended Christmas that year because Jeff wasn't there with her and she found that she missed his company. She had her kids with her and that helped fill some of the void, but she really missed him. They had spent years together and now she felt alone, especially when she saw her family members with their spouses or partners. Unlike death, she knew Jeff was still alive...and had *chosen* to be with someone else.

Awkward Relationships

Divorce can create awkward relationships where the ex-partners will stay friends with members of the family and will be asked to attend special events. When a marriage falls apart, a person will rely on his or her family for support and expect them to be on his or her "team." Even with an amicable split it can be difficult to comprehend how someone in your family could still have a relationship with your ex. In many cases the family may embrace the ex and continue to invite him or her to family gatherings. This can be very hurtful.

This situation happened to Susan. While she was married, her dad and her husband Marty developed a great friendship. Susan and Marty would always be invited to her family's house for Sunday dinner and Marty and her dad would watch football or whatever sporting event was in season. Then Susan made the announcement that her marriage was over and they were getting a divorce. Her father had issues with the divorce from the beginning and never fully accepted the fact that Marty and his daughter were no longer a couple. Susan's dad acted as if the divorce had never happened. Over a year after the divorce was final her father was still spending Sunday evenings with her ex watching sports and having dinner with him. During Thanksgiving her ex was invited to dinner as if nothing had happened even after Susan objected, asking her family not to invite him. Even though the divorce was amicable Susan felt that her family should be on her side and support her wishes.

With death this fallout never occurs.

Conclusion

Jeff was able to obtain a divorce from Veronica which allowed him to start a new life with another woman. However, he found that he not only divorced Veronica but "divorced" her family; this was made evident to him during the first Christmas holiday after the split.

Meanwhile, Veronica found that she had the painful chore of sharing the news with not only her family, but with Jeff's family as well. She was left to share the "why" and help both families understand what happened. She still felt that some members on both sides of the family believed she might not have tried hard enough. When she shared the news she felt like she had to defend herself because she thought some family members might think she was a failure or a quitter.

Painful experiences such as awkward family gatherings or resulting strained relationships are common across divorce and death. However, they vary greatly between the two because, while you know how both your family and your spouse's family would react to the death of your spouse, you don't know how they will react to the news of a divorce—they may end up feeling shock, disappointment and even their own hurt and betrayal.

Often you don't only divorce your spouse but find that you have "divorced" his or her family as well.

"The informality of family life is a blessed condition that allows us all to become our best while looking our worst."
—Marge Kennedy, Author

CHAPTER 5: FRIENDS

"Real friendship is shown in times of trouble; prosperity is full of friends." –Euripides, Ancient Greek Tragedian

Leah and Kurt met while in college where each had a great network of friends. Leah was the one who seemed to have the most friends and be more of a social butterfly. Kurt had a few friends that he hung out with, but it seemed that the couple spent most of their time at special events with Leah's friends. Eventually the day came when Kurt asked Leah to marry him and they quickly shared the joyous news with their family and friends.

They both worked professional jobs—Kurt was a lawyer and Leah was an investment advisor for a large company. They settled down into a nice home and started a family. They had two daughters, the first arriving three years after they married and the second a year later. Their family was growing and so was their social circle, although they still primarily gravitated toward and hung out with Leah's friends.

Their marriage started to deteriorate over time and the flame of their passion slowly turned into a dying ember. They reached a point when they thought it was time to tell their friends about their pending divorce. Reactions varied. Some friends took sides while others just chose to cut ties with both partners.

Both a husband and wife will usually bring a set of friends into their marriage prior to their wedding and will continue to make every attempt to stay in touch with their old friends once they marry. They will usually need to embrace some or most of the other partner's friends and accept or at least tolerate them. The couple will also make new friends during their marriage and will embrace and spend time with them as well at events and special occasions.

Over time we have all grown to depend on our friends and naturally expect them to be available to provide assistance and emotional support during traumatic events that occur in our lives—to help us feel better and offer advice.

When people lose their partners through death, the support of family and friends is sought out and expected during their time of sorrow. There is an expectation that the friends who the couple brought into the marriage and those they made during their marriage will all come together to support the grieving spouse and share condolences. Even old friends that they may not have seen in years will reach out and contact them, providing emotional encouragement and offering ways to help. During this time friends are not trying to decide which partner they should support, but instead will rally around the surviving spouse to show emotional support.

When couples divorce there seems to be an awkwardness or expectation as to how the friends of the couple should react and provide support to each partner. The expectations are often that friends should take the side of one of the partners, supporting him or her and providing moral support and validation that the ex-partner was wrong. In the end there will also be the friends who choose to distance themselves from both partners. In this situation the divorcing partners will not only have lost a spouse, but in the end will have lost friends too!

Humiliation

There will most likely be sadness and apprehension when a person makes the difficult phone call to tell a friend about the passing of his or her spouse. But there are usually no feelings of embarrassment, shame, or humiliation involved.

The expected reactions of friends when they are notified of the death can vary. Some friends react with shock or devastation while others may respond with great sorrow and deep remorse. No matter what the reaction is to the sad news, all friends will be quick to offer condolences, thoughts, and prayers. The surviving spouse, with assistance from the family, will want to inform friends as soon as possible. The one faced with the death of a spouse will not have to worry about feeling like a failure or be embarrassed.

Choosing to tell a friend about a pending divorce, however, can be a difficult conversation to have with friends. An individual going through a divorce may feel like a failure and suffer from feelings of embarrassment, shame, or humiliation because he or she couldn't keep the marriage from falling apart.

In some cases, a partner recognizes that his or her marriage is spiraling out of control and will reach out and confide in a few trusted friends who can provide support and counseling during the time leading up to the divorce. Now comes the time to tell the world and the remaining friends about the secret— the marriage is over. He or she may question or even doubt how these other friends will react to the news... *What will they think? Will they be negative and judgmental because they were the last to know? Will I be seen as a failure or a quitter?*

During the months leading up to Leah's divorce, she had shared details of the highs and lows of her deteriorating marriage with her inner circle of friends. She entertained feelings of embarrassment and shame when she thought about telling her other friends that she had not been comfortable enough to confide in them about her pending divorce.

When she finally gained courage and decided to face her fears and humiliation, she quickly told her other friends that her marriage was over. Even though she told this outer circle of friends and they responded positively, offering support, she couldn't help but feel that some of them thought she was a failure. Whether that was true or not, that was the way she felt.

Choosing Sides

Having friends choose sides is one thing that someone who has lost a spouse through death usually does not have to face. With death the only side that people take is the one of the spouse still alive. There may be dislike of the surviving spouse, but friends will provide support and stay civil out of respect of their recently deceased comrade. Choosing sides would be the last thought on anyone's mind.

In a divorce, however, friends may find themselves in an awkward position, feeling obligated to choose one partner over the other – or to not side with either, which may seem just as hurtful. The divorce can have a negative effect on those surrounding the couple because of expectations and resentments. Friendships can actually be damaged beyond repair and lost altogether as a result.

When Kurt and his wife Leah decided to divorce, he didn't really think much about how his friends would react. During the months leading up to the finalization of the divorce, Kurt started noticing that there were a few friends who started distancing themselves from him and were supporting his wife. He didn't think much about it and reconciled that there would be friends who would side with his wife and would provide their support to her. During the divorce proceedings, Kurt found himself in the middle of a nasty divorce battle. Kurt was shocked when his wife's attorney called one of his friends to testify against him, a guy that he and his wife had just celebrated with on New Year's Eve.

Kurt was devastated. He knew there would be some of his wife's friends who would take Leah's side, but he never imagined one of his close buddies would choose to testify against him in court to sway and influence the judge. Divorce was much worse than death to Kurt.

Cutting Ties

Cutting ties with friends may occur following a death of a spouse, but the thought of friends abandoning their relationship with you because of the death is not something that is expected. Breaking off a relationship with someone considered a friend, no matter how close or not, who has just lost a spouse through death would be a cold and cruel thing to do.

Divorce on the other hand is very different—some may find it too stressful to remain friends with the divorcing couple and will instead decide to break ties with both the husband and the wife rather than choose between them. Often the guilt to choose sides is thrust upon the friends by one of the divorcing partners because he or she may feel wronged and expects them to side with him or her. If the friend chooses to side with the wife instead of the husband then the friend will alienate the husband—and vice versa—often a difficult and no-win situation. So they take the easier road and cut ties.

Kurt and Leah both experienced the situation in which a set of their friends decided to choose to end their relationships with both partners. The friends cared for both Kurt and Leah and didn't want to hurt either one. The friends were well meaning and believed that by choosing to break off the relationship with both of them they wouldn't have to worry about appearing as if they were playing favorites. In most cases the friends didn't contact Kurt or Leah and just stopped visiting or responding to phone calls or chats.

No Friends

The aftermath of losing a spouse or family member through death normally does not drastically affect one's number of friends. Perhaps a few friends may fall away if they aren't that close, but the thought of someone waking up with a very small amount of friends or maybe none at all following a death is incongruent with American society.

As with family, during divorce one or both partners may find that not only did they lose each other, but they also lost friends. This could result in the tragic scenario in which one partner has very few or no friends at the end of the marriage. They slowly realize that the people with whom they had socialized during the marriage were friends that aligned with their former spouse—so when the spouse left so did the friends. They walk away from their marriage with no spouse and no friends.

The lack of friends during and after the breakup of a marriage can create a void.

Jack was someone who didn't have any friends of his own and had always hung out with his wife and her friends. During the divorce process Jack discovered that not only was his wife gone but so was his network of friends. He didn't have any male friends with whom he spent time while he and his wife were married. Since Jack didn't have any friends to help fill the vacuum left by his ex-wife, he began visiting clubs and having a few drinks as a replacement for the lack of human interaction.

To further fill the hole left in his life, Jack also quickly rebounded by remarrying not long after the divorce. He met Lisa at the bar one night and, not having any real friends, began talking to her, and they eventually went on a few dates. He was lonely after his divorce and at least Lisa was fun to be with, so he eventually asked her to marry him. For Jack, remarrying helped him fill the emptiness he felt and reinforced that someone did love him. He had to admit Lisa may not have been the perfect person to marry, but it was better than spending nights alone at the bar.

Beware of Well-Meaning Friends

We expect friends to be available to us to listen, understand, support us, provide advice and give us a different perspective on our situation. It's nice to have someone to turn to in our time of need. But one must be cautious when confiding in friends and asking them for advice when dealing with a crumbling marriage. First, most friends are not licensed therapists and are ill-equipped to give helpful advice. Second, some well-meaning friends will want to be helpful and provide feedback that will lift us up instead of being truthful for fear of hurting our feelings. Third, friends may have a negative bias against our spouse prompting them to talk us into ending our marriage instead of supporting it.

A final word of caution is to be careful when taking advice from someone who is divorced or has suffered several divorces. It's not that they can't provide good advice, because in many cases they can. But here is why caution should be used: a speaker once asked an audience, "If you were about to lose your business because you were struggling to keep it afloat, who would you seek advice from? Would you ask someone who was unsuccessful and lost their business, or someone who battled back and was successful in keeping their business intact?" The answer from the audience was, "The person who battled back." That is true for marriage too. Marriage is hard and it can be a struggle to keep it afloat, but when asking for advice, seek out and consult with someone who has had a successful track record or better yet look for a trained therapist.

Conclusion

Death and divorce are both traumatic events through which we all come to expect friends to step up and provide support. Whether it's a loss of a loved one or the loss of a dream we need friends that will cry with us, hug us, talk to us and basically be there by our sides when we are alone and dealing with a bad situation in our lives.

With the loss of a loved one we can be confident that friends will be there to support us during our time of sorrow. We would normally have no thoughts of shame and humiliation or feeling of failure because our loved ones died. Often, the one experiencing the death of a loved one can expect friends to come together to create a support group or maybe volunteer to provide meals during the week or two after the passing of the spouse. Friends are there to provide moral support during a time of grieving.

Kurt and Leah both found out first-hand the difference between death and divorce when it came to their friends. Both were faced with the situation in which a set of their friends didn't want to choose sides, so they decided to end the friendship.

On top of that, Kurt was really affected since he had fewer

friends and lost all but two of them. He also felt hurt and betrayed by his friend who testified against him, choosing his wife's side over his.

Leah worked with her inner circle of friends who mostly provided support during the crumbling of her marriage. But even though she had great support during the breakup, she still felt like some friends judged her and thought she was a failure at the marriage even though she had given it her all.

On a positive note, Kurt and Leah did learn the true meaning of friendship. Leah was able to rebound from the break-up of her marriage by engaging a close-knit group of girlfriends to help her during this period. She was able to fill the void of companionship by spending evenings and downtime with her girlfriends. She may have lost a few friends, but she received great support because her girlfriends realized how miserable and sad she had been in her existing marriage and just wanted her to be happy again. Her friends not only told her that they were available to her but made her feel confident that she could count on them for their full support during the ordeal that she was facing.

Kurt meanwhile eventually made new friends at his workplace that he still has today.

Good friends are good to have, no matter if you are single, married, widowed or divorced...and if lost, new ones can always be found. But be careful when consulting friends about a crumbling marriage. Well-meaning friends will all have advice to share—some will be helpful and some not so useful. Friends will most likely tell you what you want to hear instead of what you *need* to hear. It is best to seek out a well-meaning therapist who is trained and equipped to deal with a deteriorating marriage.

"Don't walk behind me; I may not lead. Don't walk in front of me; I may not follow. Just walk beside me and be my friend." –Unknown

CHAPTER 6: LAW

"As a lawyer, I could engage in killer litigation with the best of them. It was war, after all." –Megyn Kelly, American journalist and attorney

Tony worked as a purchasing manager for a local company and would often go for happy hour with some friends after work. One night when he was out with his friends, he noticed a lovely young woman walking into the bar with some of her friends. He introduced himself and asked her if he could buy her a drink and she agreed to a nice Pinot Noir while he ordered a beer. He found out her name was Kaye and they spent the evening chatting. Tony asked Kaye for a date and they began dating until one night during a romantic dinner, Tony asked Kaye to marry him.

Tony and Kaye moved into a nice home in the country. Tony continued working as a purchasing manager and Kaye was happy staying at home. They slowly added to their family— first with a pet dog and then with a baby boy, followed by a daughter and another son during the course of their marriage. The marriage began failing and after fifteen years they called it quits.

The divorce turned into a war with their children becoming the battleground.

There are legal processes that need to be followed whether you are faced with death or divorce including paperwork that needs to be filed and processes followed to get to legal closure in settling the estate of the deceased or in an agreement to end a marriage. The amount of paperwork needed by someone faced with divorce or death will depend on the number of assets and liabilities the couple acquired during their marriage.

Legal Process – Death

With death the processes will be somewhat predictable where the spouse or family members will have to arrange for a funeral. In some states such as Alabama the law requires that a Funeral Director be involved in the burial process. The Funeral Director can help with ordering original death certificates and contacting Social Security. The funeral and burial or cremation is the first step.

There are laws that provide processes and procedures to protect the surviving spouse to ensure they receive the assets to which they are entitled. In most cases the process will include the last will and testament of the deceased that helps the surviving family members know their loved one's last wishes and how property and financial assets should be provisioned. Another protection usually in place is that the deceased will most likely have listed his or her spouse as the beneficiary of life insurance policies, pensions, and retirement savings accounts. Normally if the couple owns property together, the surviving spouse will automatically become the sole owner of the property. There is no need to involve a lawyer since the survivor is listed on the deed.

If there is a last will and testament there is an executor that oversees this and is tasked with carrying out the wishes of the deceased. If the assets are limited to life insurance policies, pensions and jointly owned property, the will may not need to be probated or have its validity established. Also, the family members may forgo a lawyer and handle the reading of the will at a family meeting. During this time, they can agree to respect the last will and testament of the deceased. Should these be contested or complicated due to property owned solely by the deceased or by an ex-spouse still living, then the executor will need to seek out a lawyer who will schedule a meeting to guide conversations to help the family carry out the wishes of the deceased.

Once the burial and the reading of the last will and testament occurs, the surviving spouse will need to take care of several other legal requirements and will need copies of the death certificate. Many agencies require an original death certificate that contains a raised seal and not a copy as proof of death to close or modify any existing accounts the deceased may have in his or her name. If the deceased was employed at the time of death, the family member will need to reach out to the employer for assistance with gaining access to any pension plans, 401K savings plans and death benefits such as life insurance policies. The employer's human resources manager will usually advise and assist the surviving spouse with completing the forms so he or she can access funds from the various accounts. Often it is recommended but not mandatory to work with a lawyer or financial advisor to ensure that proper legal processes are followed to avoid paying unwanted taxes.

Health insurance is one of the areas that will need to also be visited especially if the surviving partner was covered under his or her spouse's medical insurance policy. If coverage was provided under the spouse's medical policy, then a new policy will need to be purchased to cover health care. Jointly held accounts such as utilities will also need to be reconciled so the name of the surviving spouse is no longer on them.

Legal Process-Divorce

There are similar legal areas that need to be handled in a divorce. The legal process for divorce can be predictable in some cases but in many instances it can become unpredictable. Either way the process begins with at least one partner filing for divorce in the local court. Whether the divorce is contested or not, forms will need to be completed to start the process, property will need to be accounted for, and, should the couple have children, they will need to be accounted for as well. One of the partners will need to appear in court as part of the legal proceeding and then based on the court's ruling in the end, the couple will be granted a divorce.

That is the simple version but in reality, divorce can be much more complex depending on whether or not it is contested.

The legal process for an uncontested divorce can be simple and, if a couple can complete their own paperwork, in most cases a lawyer will not be required. This process will vary depending on how contentious the divorcing couple becomes during the divorce process. A straightforward uncontested divorce can be short, quick, and somewhat painless if the couple has mutually agreed to end their marriage. At least one spouse has to have valid, legal reason to ask the court to sever the marriage and grant a divorce. In some states like Maryland, mutual consent can be a legal reason or grounds to seek a divorce.

The process starts with at least one partner completing the appropriate forms and then filing them in local court. The couple will be required to complete, sign, and submit a settlement agreement that outlines the care for the children, spousal support, and distribution of property with these forms. The court in Maryland has a requirement that the spouse filing for divorce must ensure that his or her spouse is served a summons. One of the divorcing partners will need to appear in court on the day of the hearing to finalize the divorce. At this point the marriage has legally come to an end where each partner is free to remarry someone else.

But a contested divorce is much more complicated. It too starts with one partner filing the paperwork to start the process, but what happens next can be wildly unpredictable. If the couple cannot come to an agreement on how to distribute their assets or decide who will provide custody for their children, or if they each believe they have a lot to lose, then the battling partners will most likely hire lawyers.

Custody-Death

Some of the issues that are at stake for the divorcing couple will normally not be factors for someone who has lost a spouse due to death. Death and divorce differ in three basic areas: the first is focused on the wellbeing of minor children. Normally the one issue that someone who loses a spouse through death doesn't have to worry about is who will retain custody of the surviving children.

Unless the surviving parent is negligent in the treatment of the children, there is rarely a custody case involving the surviving children in the case of a death. The surviving parent will have sole custody of the children by default without any legal proceedings. (There are cases, however, in which the deceased had sole custody of the children from a previous marriage where the surviving ex-partner may file for custody of the children, but this is usually not contested.)

Custody-Divorce

With divorce, however, the custody of minor children, especially involving young children who cannot make a legal decision, will need to be discussed and settled. Children become part of the legal system during the divorce proceedings just like any other property or assets over which the divorcing couple is fighting. The courts are concerned with the wellbeing of the children during and after the divorce.

Sometimes the discussion of custody is simple—the parents agree on the arrangements for their children and provide a written outline as to what has been agreed upon. There are cases where the couple will keep it simple but will include their lawyers in the discussion who can serve as mediators to help assuage their fears by helping them see that they are not being railroaded or swindled.

But sometimes, unfortunately, custody is far more complex, combative and costly.

Should the divorcing couple not be able to come to a quick compromise on custody, their lawyers will draw up battle plans to fight on behalf of each partner to gain custody of the children based on their clients' desires.

Children can become pawns used to gain leverage; often a parent will try and win them to his or her side and demonize the other parent. Custody cases can become messy where the couple's minor children will be requested to speak in court to help the judge understand and make a ruling as to which parent should get custody of the children.

The process during the court hearings for the children usually involves more than a judge and the couple's lawyers. Others can include investigators needed to follow-up on any accusations that may have been lobbed at the opposing spouses, therapists who may be called upon to interview children to understand their mindsets and to provide a report to the judge assisting with the custody decision, and sometimes the children need their own lawyer to represent them, which the court can assign.

In some cases, even after the custody arrangements have been agreed or ruled upon and the divorce has been finalized, there may be ongoing battles where an ex-partner may change his or her mind and request a different custody arrangement— and a new court case is opened up again.

When Tony and his wife Kaye couldn't agree on custody of their three minor children, the family's case found its way into the court system where the presiding judge had to decide which parent would gain custody. Tony was asking for joint custody, but his wife wanted full custody and during the deliberations in court neither lawyer was able to make a convincing argument for either side to help the judge make a decision. So the judge ordered that the children would meet with a therapist who would interview each child and then complete a report on the findings which she would then submit to the judge.

The report submitted by the therapist advised that Tony and his wife should have joint custody of the children. Tony was very pleased with the therapist's report, but his joy was short lived when the judge decided to award Kaye full custody of the children.

Tony filed an appeal to have the judge's ruling overturned since a licensed therapist had recommended joint custody. In his appeal he made note that Kaye didn't want him listed as a parent on any paperwork at the children's school. Kaye seemed to be very insecure as a parent since she was always concerned that the children may show more love to their dad instead of her. Tony felt he had a valid appeal and believed that his children needed both a mom and dad. Instead Tony lost his appeal and he was crushed.

Spousal Support

Spousal support can cause the divorce to become messy and complicated, and of course this is a topic that doesn't concern someone who has lost a spouse through death. In some instances, a partner may want to give everything up while in an emotional state of guilt, apathy or surrender, just to make it all "go away."

The lawyer can provide a sanity check to help an exhausted partner avoid making a decision based on short-term vision that may have long-term regrets.

Should both partners have similar incomes then the divorce process shouldn't become very complicated and both can agree that no spousal support is required. However, should there be a disparity between the partner's incomes the lawyer can provide advice and request that the partner with the higher income provide support.

Property

The third and final area of contention that will complicate the legal process will be the division of assets or property. The more assets that a couple brings into divorce court, the more complicated the process will be if the couple can't agree. Assets are just one of the areas in which a couple may have a lot to lose and will be willing to fight. In most situations both partners will hire a lawyer to help work out the details of a fair division of property.

There are many determining factors that affect the distribution of assets, for example, if a property is owned by one spouse prior to the marriage as opposed to it being accumulated during the marriage. Real estate, bank accounts, and cars are just a few examples of assets a couple may have to compromise on to determine which partner will gain access or ownership. If the couple cannot agree on how they will share and divide the properties in question, then their legal teams will stay busy working with the couple sorting it out.

Dena thought her divorce would be relatively simple when it came to the property that she and her husband John owned jointly. They had a beautiful house and several automobiles and they had made arrangements for Dena to gain possession of the home and cars. Dena thought she could work with her husband without involving a lawyer but John changed his mind about giving her any assets and Dena had to go to court.

She had to work with her lawyer to gain use and possession of the home for her and their children since she had previously won sole custody of them. The lawyer helped Dena persuade John to stay with the original agreement and to allow Dena to have possession of the cars as well. But even once she was able to gain possession of the automobiles, she had to work with her lawyer to have John provide her with proof of ownership so she could purchase auto insurance. She continued to work with her attorney to ensure that all of their assets listed the name of the person who had current ownership and responsibility for them after the divorce.

Chris didn't fare so well when the topic of property was discussed between him and his ex-wife Melinda. They couldn't agree on the best approach for the house and had to rely on the court to make a decision. Because Melinda maintained sole custody of the children, she was awarded the family home. Chris found that the divorce process was lengthy but was surprised when he was told that he had to vacate the home within just thirty days. Of course he worked with his lawyer to get an extension but the judge denied it. He had to quickly find a new place to live and move his belongings out of the house. A process that lasted so long seemed to end so very abruptly.

Conclusion

The legal proceedings include processes and procedures that are designed to provide guidance for anyone faced with the death of a spouse...or death of a dream. Someone faced with either situation can find assistance to help them during the process. A funeral director or human resources person can assist with the legal affairs when one is faced with death of a loved one. Some states will offer assistance and there are websites that can provide aid to anyone who has the question, "How do I end my marriage?" In some instances paperwork can be completed without the assistance of a lawyer to settle the accounts of a decedent or the development of a settlement statement dealing with divorce. However, someone may want to hire a lawyer to handle a couple's assets based on the complication of the will or the lack of a compromise between a divorcing couple.

The similarities between death and divorce change when the topic turns to custody of children, spousal support, and distribution of assets.

With a death, the legal system covers the surviving spouse; in most cases he or she is expected to maintain custody of minor children and take ownership of the assets. Spousal support isn't a concern since there is no spouse to seek support.

Divorce on the other hand is not as straightforward even if the two divorcing partners have previously agreed on spousal support and distribution of the assets and minor children. Depending on how high the stakes are, the couple will most likely both hire lawyers creating a battleground where the partners will fight to win what they believe is rightfully theirs.

Dena's divorce process went fairly well with a few hiccups, but she was able to work those out with the assistance of a lawyer. The attorney served as a mediator between Dena and her husband John to help keep them on track and execute the original settlement that they had agreed to at the start of the divorce. They were both able to agree on custody and spousal support since Dena wanted independence and had an income that was equivalent to John's. There was a brief breakdown in communications in regard to distributing the assets but with the assistance of a lawyer they were able to come to an agreement with very little pain.

The legal process can be very complicated for divorce or death, but if all involved in the process can compromise on difficult issues should they arise, then it can be somewhat painless.

There are self-help websites offered by some states such as Maryland and of course there are many websites dedicated to divorce and death that will provide assistance and advice. In most areas there is free legal help available to anyone who has the question, "How do I end my marriage?"

Some local courts may offer free assistance by helping to complete the required forms and may have people on staff who can help decipher the law and explain the rights of the one seeking the divorce. The state of Maryland provides access to a free lawyer that can act in an advisory role to anyone contacting the local Family Law Self-Help Center or Maryland Courts Self-Help Center. The staff can help set and manage expectations as to what someone can expect during divorce proceedings based on whether the divorce is uncontested or contested.

There is also help that can be found on the Internet from companies that will assist people in completing forms, but of course this comes with a fee.

"Wouldn't it be great if every marriage could come with a guarantee of a 'happily ever after'?" – John Logan, CEO, SafeGuard Guaranty

CHAPTER 7: FINANCES

"Divorce is an expensive punishment love gets when it fails" —Bangambiki Habyarimana, Author

Leon and Jessica dated for about three years before finally deciding to get married. Their wedding was held at a beautiful venue where they were surrounded by family and friends. They both were employed with modest incomes and saved money for a down payment to purchase a home in a nice suburban neighborhood. They decided to start a family and had a son four years into the marriage and then a daughter three years later, adding a Golden Retriever to round out their unit, becoming what many consider the "All-American family."

With a growing family they decided to sell their starter home and buy a larger house to accommodate their needs with a yard and plenty of room for the children to run and play. The purchase of the home came with monthly mortgage payments that were affordable for the couple.

Ready to celebrate eight years of marriage, Leon and Jessica seemed to have it all, everything anyone would want in life. They had two beautiful kids, great jobs with good incomes, a beautiful home, and a family dog. To everyone looking in from the outside, Leon and Jessica were truly living the American dream.

But on the inside, the couple argued and fought all the time. They considered marriage counseling but could never find the time with both kids playing various sports and all of their extracurricular activities.

Then their marriage crashed like the stock market and was just as financially devastating. Jessica filed for divorce.

Financial impacts can have serious consequences on a family whether they happen as a result of the death of a spouse or with the breakup of a marriage. In today's society both spouses are normally employed and in many cases need to be because the salaries of both are required to meet financial obligations such as paying the mortgage, insurance, health costs, utility bills, keeping two cars in the garage, putting food on the table, going on vacation...the list goes on. Normally the loss of a partner's income can be disastrous since both salaries are required to pay for a home and maintain the desirable lifestyle to which each partner has grown accustomed.

There are costs associated with death and divorce that will need to be tallied and resolved. However, the financial costs of losing someone by death are normally predictable and most major expenses at the time of death consist of one-time fees such as funeral costs. The costs of divorce can be unpredictable, however, and in some cases continue long after the divorce has been finalized.

Safety Net

A big difference between death and divorce is that people are taught to prepare for death and part of the preparation is to have some type of financial safety net to protect the family. Often there is a life insurance package that has been purchased for this purpose to help cover the financial loss of the spouse's salary. In many cases this insurance may help to pay off the mortgage of the family home. In addition to life insurance, there are also government assistance programs that are available to help augment the salary of the deceased spouse. The assistance normally comes in the form of Social Security benefits which will pay the surviving spouse some funds and provide financial assistance to fund the children's college program.

There usually is no benefit package or safety net such as a life insurance policy or social security, however, to help offset the costs of divorce. Many times the divorced partners find themselves in a situation where they are forced to continue to live together while the divorce is being processed so they can use both incomes to pay the mortgage until they can sell the house. This can add even more stress and hardship to an already deteriorating family situation.

Financial assistance may come in the form of family or friends but there is very little federal and state financial aid to help the divorcing couple. The only finances that are readily available are their salaries and any financial assets such as real estate, retirement accounts, and savings accounts—but they are usually frozen and unavailable in a contentious breakup as soon as the divorce papers are filed.

Insurance – Death

Planning for death is something that we are all taught in life. Everyone knows that they will die someday, so a wise and loving person will have developed a financial plan to care for the family in the event of his or her death to help offset the loss of an income. Life insurance is one of the tools in the financial "toolbox" to have in case of death to help offset costs. Many employers offer life insurance packages to their employees to purchase to ensure their families are cared for in case of the loss of income. A life insurance policy may also help offset the cost of funeral expenses.

When someone purchases a home in the United States, the purchaser will be bombarded by insurance companies with offers to cover the cost of the mortgage should the purchaser die prior to paying off the mortgage. This is a benefit for the surviving spouse so there will be no concerns or worries. These insurance policies help provide peace of mind at the time of a tragic event so the family doesn't have to be concerned over financial funds which would add to the burdens of loss they already face.

I remember when I first entered into the workforce; my company offered a life insurance policy that I could purchase at a reasonable price. I took advantage of that opportunity and when I purchased my first home, I increased the value to at least cover the cost of paying off my mortgage. The reason was simple: I didn't know when I would die but that someday I would, and I wanted to ensure that my family was not burdened with my debts. I knew without the insurance, my family members who were already strapped for cash would not be able to make my mortgage payments and would have to immediately sell the house.

My dad didn't own a home but had a life insurance policy that covered his burial. I was very grateful to my dad that he had planned for his own death and had purchased the policy. The funds were enough to cover his funeral expenses and thankfully he did not have other debts to cover. If he had died with a mortgage on a house or had other sizeable debts, his death would have been financially devastating for us.

Insurance – Divorce

Divorce is different. During the engagement phase of a marriage, there are many things to plan and schedule that are designed to help make the wedding day a special event when the loving couple says their "I do's." One thought that will probably never cross their minds is the need to take out an insurance policy to cover their losses should they divorce. Why should they, since most traditional wedding vows contain the phrase "till death do us part" with each partner committing to spend the rest of their lives together? The loving couple has no thoughts of divorce.

The thought of purchasing a marriage insurance policy to cover the chance that they might divorce someday would appear as if the couple is planning for their marriage to fail. The only plans that the two love birds have on their minds is planning a life together, making dreams come true, and growing old together.

And yet, at one time in the United States there was such a

product—an insurance company that had started offering Divorce Insurance for couples. That company was SafeGuard Guaranty Corporation which introduced its divorce insurance policy called Wedlock Divorce Insurance. The concept was completely new compared to other types of insurance policies that a couple might ordinarily purchase during their marriage. Divorce insurance was designed to provide a payout to the policyholder once the divorce was finalized to help that individual from facing financial ruin after the divorce.

However, according to John Logan, CEO of SafeGuard Guaranty, in 2012 the US insurance regulators outlawed divorce insurance products such as Wedlock as well as a proposed new and improved product called Marriage Assurance. Logan said that while the changes to two obscure laws were made in the guise of protecting financial risk to consumers, the changes in the laws impacted only one company in the entire industry negatively—SafeGuard Guaranty—and anyone who might come afterward offering a similar type of policy. Every other insurance company that had an existing product that would have had to comply with the new regulations was "grandfathered," meaning they were exempt from any negative impact in perpetuity, Logan said. All existing divorce policies purchased through SafeGuard's website were subsequently canceled and paid-in premiums were returned to the policyholders.

Today, divorce insurance cannot be purchased anywhere in the world. But Egypt is considering making such a policy mandatory for couples to obtain before they get married. Still, no one anywhere is offering it yet and obtaining such a policy in the US is now out of the question until the laws change.

While the thought of divorce insurance may sound odd, it seems to make financial sense for a married couple given the statistics of what usually occurs after a divorce: 44% of women in the US go below the poverty line for some period of time; 60% of the people in the US currently under the poverty line are divorced women with children; and, according to Logan, $112 billion dollars would be saved annually by federal, state and local taxpayers if divorce insurance policies were executed.

Statistics also show the odds of a US couple divorcing during their lifetime are greater than the odds of someone being involved in an automobile accident (one in three people divorce while only one in four get in car accidents). And yet auto insurance is mandatory and divorce insurance is now illegal.

Even if divorce insurance had been available for Jessica and Leon to purchase, the thought of getting divorced had never crossed their minds during their marriage. Why would they have thoughts of divorce? They had purchased a new home a year prior to splitting. So the only forms of financial assistance available to the former lovers now facing divorce was to reach out to their parents for a loan, withdraw money from their 401K plans, use their credit cards or, since they owned a house, sell their home and split the proceeds to help finance the rest of the divorce expenses and find adequate housing for each of them and the children. The only other option was to have the home appraised and if there was enough equity in it, have it refinanced as long as the spouse keeping the home could afford the monthly payments. This would serve two purposes by providing cash to "buy out" the other partner and remove his or her name from the deed.

Federal Assistance

One financial assistance program that is available at death but is not readily available with divorce is Social Security. This benefit system is an important government tool to help families after the death of a spouse. The family may be able to collect Social Security benefits to help offset the loss of income with hopes of keeping the family financially solvent. Social security is not available to someone divorcing until they reach a particular age and the benefit is only available to the spouse and not the children.

There are government funded programs in the United States available to a parent that has experienced a loss through death or divorce to help offset some of the loss of income from a spouse's salary. But too often the standard of living drops, often below the poverty line. Government programs such as the Children's Health Insurance Program (CHIP) coupled with Medicaid can assist with the healthcare of children.

Housing is of great concern when someone finds themselves in a position where there is no longer two incomes and one is insufficient to fund affordable housing. Normally a couple will have a mortgage or monthly rent payment that requires both of their incomes to maintain the desired lifestyle. The good news for someone in this position is that there is a federal government housing choice voucher program that can provide housing assistance to low-income families.

Whether it occurs through death or divorce, parents have another concern when they find themselves in a single status—finding affordable, trustworthy childcare for their children while they are at work. The cost of childcare can be very expensive and in many cases, can consume the salary of one partner leaving the couple to rely on the salary of the other partner to pay the bills. However, a single parent doesn't have the luxury of having a second income to offset the basic financial costs that every household experiences. The single salary may be insufficient when it comes to covering both the cost of childcare and the cost of housing. Fortunately, there are federal and state childcare programs available for single parents, but they must meet certain parameters.

Once they began their split, Jessica and Leon were not able to take advantage of the state programs due to their incomes being too high or sufficient to support them.

Teresa on the other hand was able to take advantage of the subsidized healthcare, childcare, and housing programs available. Teresa and her husband Dave had found a nice townhome to rent that was close to work and allowed their two children to attend the nearby school. They were pleased with their landlord and were both comfortable being in a position to pay the rent. The children enjoyed the new home because they had their own bedrooms and their friends lived in the same community. Teresa and Dave's marriage began falling apart, however, and he moved out of the townhome leaving Teresa with the kids and the rent payment. Teresa was very concerned since she and her husband had both signed the lease for the townhome and she needed a place to live where the kids could continue going to school.

Teresa called several state agencies to inquire about assistance and discovered that there was financial aid to help her with childcare and housing. After the divorce, she reached out to her local housing voucher program to request assistance to pay her rent and assist with utilities. She didn't want to move and was hoping to be able to stay in the house that she and her husband had leased. Based on her single salary, the program agreed to provide a voucher that would be paid to the landlord to cover half the rent and assist with utilities. She explained to the landlord that she was getting divorced but she had found financial assistance to compensate her husband's portion of the rent. The landlord agreed and Teresa and her children were able to continue living in the home, plus she was able to stay on at her job which she enjoyed.

Formal Process Costs

The financial costs that someone will incur during the "beginning to end" process to say "good-bye" to someone will vary with death and divorce.

The burial process for death normally takes three to four days or less and the costs are usually predictable. Costs for a funeral or what is often referred to these days as a "celebration of life" vary throughout the country and depend on how much money the family wishes to spend or can afford. During the planning phase of the funeral the family will work with a funeral director or associate to help determine what amenities, features, and options the family wishes to arrange for their loved one. They usually entail a selection of a casket or urn, viewings, religious preferences, and whether there will be a burial in a cemetery or cremation. Often times the family may splurge to have a catered meal with family and friends afterward.

When Linda's mother passed away in 2018, the funeral coats were approximately $12,000 which included a medium-priced casket, the use of the funeral home for a viewing and use of the chapel for hosting the celebration of life. It didn't include the cemetery lot which was an additional $3,000 and her family had to spend another $1,000 for personnel to be on hand to open and close the grave. Because the funeral was on a Saturday Linda's family had to pay an additional fee to cover weekend services at $650 per hour. But the overall cost for the funeral and burial was a one-time fee.

Divorce Costs

There is no celebration of life ceremony (or usually any other kind) with divorce but the beginning to end process can take several months, a year, or several years and in some cases continues even after the couple has officially said good-bye to their marriage.

The process for divorce typically consists of filing for divorce, lots of paperwork, a court hearing or multiple hearings and sometimes a whole lot more before the divorce is eventually finalized. If the partners don't agree to compromise through mediation, then the financial costs for divorce can be unpredictable depending on attorneys' fees and multiple meetings and hearings.

The cost of a divorce can vary as to whether someone chooses the Do It Yourself (DIY) divorce route or needs to involve a lawyer in the process. If a couple can come to a mutual agreement and can agree on the major issues, then an uncontested divorce is less expensive and allows the couple to take the DIY divorce route. In Maryland, the process starts with at least one partner completing the appropriate forms and then filing the papers in local court. The couple will be required to submit a settlement agreement that outlines the care for the children, spousal support, and distribution of property with these forms. The filing fee in Maryland is a straight $165 with a process for waiving the filing fee based on a person's financial situation. After filing, there may still be the need for $50 to cover the costs to hire someone to serve the spouse with the divorce papers. The total cost of the divorce can be under $500.

Maryland provides anyone seeking a divorce with free assistance to complete the necessary forms if they contact the Maryland Courts Self-Help Center. There are also websites that provide a document preparation service to help with the completion of all of the forms required for each state. The assistance comes with a $299 flat fee and the couple carries the responsibility for filing the completed forms at their local courthouse and paying the court fees.

Sometimes a couple may need some additional assistance with drafting the settlement agreement. The couple can work with an impartial divorce mediator that works on behalf of both parties to negotiate a settlement that both parties can agree on and submit to the court. The cost is normally shared by both parties and the mediator works with the couple to draft a satisfactory agreement on how to share assets including children if involved. If someone can't afford the mediation fees, there "are some court, government, and community programs that may provide mediation services based on a sliding scale or for free." (The People's Law Library of Maryland 2019).

In Maryland, the cost of a private divorce mediator can vary based on the length of the discussions. Normally sessions can take two to three hours but can last longer based on the complexity of the issues. However, at any time the divorcing couple can't agree and come to a compromise, the divorce becomes a "contested" one and the costs can escalate quickly and become very unpredictable.

The lack of compromise and agreement can become uncivil, involving lawyers and possible custody hearings if the couple has children. In some cases the costs can skyrocket leaving some wondering if the financial bleeding will ever stop. The individual cost of divorce in Maryland typically ranges from $4,000 to $28,000 if attorneys are involved. The average total cost is $14,000 with the average attorney's fees making up

$11,000 of the $14,000. If a couple has considerable assets such as property and retirement accounts, or if there is a heated custody battle, the average cost can be around $35,000.

Major Categories Affecting Costs

There are three major categories affecting costs with divorce that are normally never discussed when someone loses a spouse through death. Of course, if the divorcing couple can come to a compromise on these three and never need the court to settle the dispute, the costs will be significantly less.

The first category that can drive up the price of divorce fifty percent or more over the average divorce cost concerns minor children. The more complicated the child custody case involving lawyers, investigators, and therapists, the higher the costs can climb exponentially. Some of the costs that may need to be covered during custody trials are childcare, attorneys' and investigative fees, communication, travel and witness expenses.

The second category that will increase the average cost of divorce is the request for financial support such as spousal support or alimony and child support if children are involved.

Third, settling property issues can sometimes be the biggest boost in the increase in the cost of a divorce based on the quality and quantity of assets that needs to be divided between the divorcing couple. The more financial assets a couple has acquired during their marriage, the more complicated and costly that divorce becomes.

JoAnn and Larry had been married eight years and had two children and a home with a mortgage. JoAnn explained that she wanted out of the marriage and that they could keep the cost of the divorce to less than $500, but they would both have to agree on a settlement that covered all of their assets including the children. Larry acquiesced to a divorce on the grounds of mutual consent and they were able to sign the required court ordered settlement forms agreeing to split the proceeds from the sale of the house. Because Larry and JoAnn were able to compromise on assets and custody of the children, they were able to keep the costs under $500.

Leon and Jessica were not as fortunate. Jessica filed the divorce paperwork and had Leon served with the divorce papers which shocked him since he wanted the marriage to work. Jessica had stated that they could keep the divorce costs to less than $500 if lawyers weren't involved because a lawyer would cost an average of $15,000 each. But Leon couldn't fully agree with Jessica's terms and decided that the DIY route would not work; he hired a lawyer to represent him which prompted Jessica to hire a lawyer as well.

There was no argument over who should keep the house because both salaries were required to pay the mortgage; they agreed to sell it since they both wanted the profits from the equity. They sought out a realtor to list and sell their family home which they had only purchased a year earlier.

But they were disappointed when the realtor told them the list price; the market price of the house had not increased significantly over the previous year since they had purchased it. They were not able to recoup the realtor fees nor the money they had invested in making several improvements, so they lost several thousand dollars. They were able to each walk away with some cash from the sale of the house, but the family home that they had saved money to buy was now gone, just like their marriage.

For Tony and Kaye, the divorce process turned even uglier and much more costly when the time came to divvy up the children. The divorce became very expensive when it went to court and the attorney's fees mounted. Tony ended up being responsible for paying all of the costs which exceeded over $100,000 with custody battles and the appeal which he lost in the end. On top of that the judge ruled that the children should be interviewed by a licensed therapist to help determine who should gain custody; the therapist presented the judge with a 35-page report and presented Tony with an additional bill of $10,000 for her services.

Financial Advisor

Tatyana Bunich of Financial 1 Wealth Management Group advocates scheduling a meeting with a financial advisor with post-divorce finance experience once the divorce is final. She recommends waiting because up until then the partners are either working between themselves or are working with their lawyer or mediator to assist them with developing a final settlement. A financial advisor can assess the post-divorce financial status of the new divorcee to protect against possible tax issues after settlement and review financial accounts, retirement plans, and current life insurance policies to ensure the ex is no longer a beneficiary or joint owner on any accounts. If there are children, it is also important to discuss the creation of a will and last testament to protect estate inheritance especially in the case of remarriage.

Religious Ramifications

Depending on how observant a person is of their faith and their religious beliefs there may be additional costs incurred other than the costs of the civil divorce process. Based on a person's faith there may be a requirement to annul or invalidate the marriage or complete a formal religious divorce process.

In the Catholic Church, should one of the partners choose to remarry someone new and wish for a wedding ceremony in the Church, he or she will need to file an annulment declaring the previous marriage invalid. The cost of an annulment can range from $500 to $1,000.

Jewish law on the other hand requires the termination of the marriage by a formal religious divorce called a *get*. In Judaism the woman will need to receive a *get* from her husband and once she accepts, the couple will be free to remarry. The *get* process usually costs less than $500.

GoFundMe

In today's society there is another means to fund the costs of a divorce or death. GoFundme is a popular method of soliciting donations for a variety of charitable causes including everything from assistance with medical or healthcare costs for patients to the purchase of school supplies by teachers. GoFundme sites are also often used to help solicit donations for families that have lost a loved one through death to help offset the funeral, children's tuition, and other costs typically incurred due to the untimely loss of a loved one.

For example, the recent tragedy of a firefighter who died as a hero attempting to put out a fire caused his family to experience an untimely loss and financial burden that they weren't prepared to handle. A Gofundme site was created to allow families, friends, and strangers to donate to the fireman's fund to help offset the funeral costs and provide tuition assistance for his children. Many people, some of whom had never even met the fireman, donated to the GoFundMe site providing the family with financial assistance.

What about a GoFundMe site to help pay for your divorce? There are now GoFundMe sites that have been set up soliciting monetary assistance to help with the costs of divorce. The GoFundMe sites for divorce include victims of abusive marriages asking for assistance to fund their divorces so they can escape, spouses who are fighting for custody of their children, and even those asking for financial help to finance their soon-to-be-ex-spouse's portion of the divorce to convince him or her to agree to it.

But the responses to the GoFundMe requests are not very well supported and these sites are often viewed as scams. Unlike a GoFundMe site for financial assistance with a death, there seems to be a lack of sympathy when a request is being made for donations to offset the costs of divorce. The request to help with lawyer costs in a divorce seems to fall on deaf ears since divorce is seen as a choice and there isn't the same type of urgency as with death. In most cases the requester will only receive donations to cover a fraction of the costs that are being solicited if anything at all.

Conclusion

Death and divorce both can result in financial ramifications on the lives of those left behind. The major difference between death and divorce is that death is certain while divorce may never occur in a marriage.

A responsible person who has a family will plan to have a life insurance policy to help offset the financial loss that results. But the last thought on the mind of two loving people when they get married is the thought of marriage insurance to help offset the costs of divorce. If they did consider it, they would be admitting the presumed failure of their marriage at the start.

Death and divorce will have a price tag. The price for death will be somewhat predictable with the costs not fluctuating very much during the process. The costs for divorce can be somewhat predictable but can also quickly become unpredictable and can wildly escalate should the divorce become contested and/or the couple not be able to agree on a settlement without involving lawyers.

There are government funded financial assistance programs that are available to families that are suffering a loss through death or divorce. These benefits may be able to offset the costs of housing, childcare and medical care for the children. Each state's program may vary so check with the state in which you reside to determine what is available.

"It's good to have money and the things that money can buy, but it's good, too, to check up once in a while and make sure that you haven't lost the things that money can't buy."
— George Lorimer, American journalist, author and publisher

CHAPTER 8: FAITH

"For I hate divorce!' says the LORD" –Malachi 2:16 (NLT)

Jane was out with her friend Carrie for a girl's night out at a local bar. While at the bar, Carrie bumped into an old friend named Matt and introduced him to Jane. Matt and Jane struck up a conversation and hit it off, leading Matt to ask her out on a date the following week to watch a movie. After that they began dating and would often get together and hang out with some of Matt's buddies at their favorite bar. One day instead of going to the bar, Matt decided to stop for lunch at their favorite restaurant and Matt asked Jane to marry him; she said yes. They had a small wedding with a few close friends at a local church. They quickly settled into a home and two years later they had a son named Stephen. Matt worked in construction and Jane worked for the state government.

Their marriage started going downhill not long after Stephen was born. It wasn't a fast slide but more like a slow fall. When he wasn't at home, Matt would spend time with his buddies at the bar drinking and playing cards. His friends were his main focus. Jane slowly started to realize that she had never been his best friend and that she was number two in his life with his buddies collectively taking the number one spot.

Even though Jane and her husband were living in the same house, she began experiencing loneliness even when they were physically together. Jane was struggling in her marriage and had developed a very unhealthy low self-esteem as a result, leaving her depressed most of the time. She realized the negative effects that her husband's neglect and abandonment and their unhealthy marriage were having on her and she began taking steps to work on herself to improve her self-worth. She started exercising and going to the gym to get fit physically and mentally to help improve her outlook and self-image. She also began eating healthier and losing weight in hopes of making herself more attractive to her husband so he would hang around the house more.

But all of her efforts didn't make any difference in the way her husband treated her. His actions didn't change. He continued to spend his free time at the bar with his buddies. When she complained, Matt would respond that she knew who he was when she married him and he wasn't about to change anytime soon.

Jane was invited on a girl's night out by some of her girlfriends. While she was out with her friends she was introduced to a good-looking, kind and interesting guy her age named Barry, and the two connected. Barry slowly became Jane's best friend and she became his. Having Barry in her life made her see there was another world in which she wasn't lonely but felt attractive, desirable and appreciated. He filled the void that she currently felt with her husband. Her new best friend gave her the strength to help her realize that she wasn't alone, allowing her to make the painful decision to ask her husband for a divorce.

Leading up to the decision to ask Matt for a divorce, Jane struggled with guilt over the choice to end her marriage. She got separated and started dating Barry and they eventually married.

But Jane's upbringing in her church made her afraid that people would not forgive her for what she had done. Worse, she felt that God would not forgive her because she believed divorce was a sin and had chosen to end her marriage anyway. Jane knew that she had to tell her family that she had asked her husband for a divorce but didn't know how they would handle the news.

Her first worry was that members of her family who were devout Protestants would not be happy about the news, especially since she had asked her husband for the divorce instead of the other way around. She felt that her family would judge her and think less of her because she gave up on her marriage. She finally worked up the courage to tell them.

Faith and Marriage

Faith can play an important role in the decisions people make throughout their lives; it is a major source that helps them become who they are and sustains them during the good and bad times. Many people look to their faith as a guiding light to help with the decisions they make during their lifetime. So faith naturally plays a major role in marriage and can be a deciding factor in who a person marries.

If two people who are interested in one another are not of the same faith it can pose problems going forward. Faith can affect the little things in a relationship and marriage, such as determining the venue of the wedding ceremony. Couples have to decide whether to be wed in a church, synagogue, mosque, or a non-religious venue such as the local courthouse. And it can affect big things such as how they spiritually raise their children.

A marriage is often deeply rooted in one's faith and depending on that faith, it is believed in many cases that a marriage union is sanctioned by God. Marriage is condoned and supported by most major religions as an important or even necessary part of life.

Christians believe that when two people marry, they are making a covenant with God to spend the rest of their lives with one another with the purpose of not only starting a life and dream together but starting a family. Catholics believe that marriage is one of the seven Holy Sacraments and are required to go through Pre-Cana counseling by a deacon or priest before they say their vows in a Catholic church.

A Muslim husband and wife will sign a "nikah" which is a contract to enter into matrimony and to fulfill its responsibilities. Islam encourages raising one's children in accordance with the Islamic faith, but it is not necessarily part of the nikah contract.

In Judaism, the "ketubah" is a marriage contract signed by two witnesses. While traditional Jews still use the ketuba containing the groom's obligations to his bride, more liberal forms of Judaism see it as an agreement between the groom and bride outlining the couple's responsibility to each other.

Christianity

Christians believe that marriage is a covenant between the groom, bride and God. The belief is that they are making a promise before God to love and cherish the individuals they are marrying. The Christian wedding vows contain the words "until death do us part" where two people make a vow before God and family that they will stay married until separated by death.

The Christian ceremony can be a large celebration with family and friends in attendance or the marriage ceremony may occur in a judge's office.

Even though the marriage performed outside a church is legal and binding there are some who believe that a church wedding is required for the marriage to be legal in the eyes of God.

In fact, the Catholic Church deems that the marriage of two Catholics is only valid if it is held in a Catholic church. The marriage of a Catholic couple outside the Church without a dispensation may have legal standing in the eyes of the state, but it has no legitimate standing in the eyes of the Church and in fact, the couple is considered to be living in sin.

The Bible is viewed as the infallible word of God. In the Gospel of Mark in the Bible Jesus is recorded as saying, *"But at the beginning of creation God made them male and female. 'For this reason, a man will leave his father and mother and be united to his wife, and the two will become one flesh. So they are no longer two, but one. Therefore, what God has joined together, let no one separate'."* (Mark 10:6-9. NIV)

Islam

Marriage is an essential part of life in the Islamic faith. Muslims sign a nikah or marriage contract between the husband and wife outlining their responsibilities to each other. The wedding can, but doesn't have to, take place in a Mosque or be officiated by an Imam and can be conducted anywhere and by anyone. The nikah is the actual Muslim wedding ceremony, but in the United States the couple will also require a civil marriage as well.

The purpose of an Islamic marriage is to join a couple together so they can build a life and cherish each other for the rest of their lives while also raising children in the Muslim faith. Marriage provides stability and spiritual support, especially for procreation. However, although Islam encourages raising one's children in accordance with the Islamic faith, it is not necessarily part of the nikah contract.

As a source of authority, the Muslims have the Qur'an which was revealed to the Prophet Muhammad, the book they believe to be the word of Allah. The Qur'an contains the teachings on marriage for the Muslim: *"And among His signs is this, that He created for you mates from among yourselves, that you may dwell in peace and tranquility with them, and He has put love and mercy between your hearts."* (Qur'an 30:21)

Judaism

Marriage is very important for Jews and is viewed as an action that pleases God where two people unite for life to start a family and raise children in the Jewish faith. The act of marriage has deep ties to Judaism as something a person is to do in obedience to God where two people become the soul of one.

An integral part of a Jewish wedding ceremony is the ketubah, a marriage contract that is witnessed by two people of the faith. "The ketubah is a unilateral agreement drawn by witnesses in accordance with Jewish civil law, in which they testify that the husband guarantees to his wife that he will meet certain minimum human and financial conditions of marriage,"

Maurice Lamm states in his book, *The Jewish Way in Love and Marriage.*

Today the ketubah doesn't just contain the groom's obligations toward his bride, but instead includes the vows the groom and bride are making toward each other. For guidance, the Jewish people have the Torah which is a source of authority on marriage. Genesis 2:24 (NIV) states, *"That is why a man leaves his father and mother and is united to his wife, and they become one flesh."*

Faith and Divorce

Faith also usually plays a big role in death and divorce. Death is straightforward. When we hear of someone dying, we don't naturally think about someone having to make a decision to terminate the life of the loved one. There are times when a decision has to be made but this is not a common thought with the death of a loved one. Most of the time death just occurs and is a natural process. When we hear of someone dying we don't ask, "Was it a painful decision?" There is also no stigma or remarriage issues with the death of a spouse. No one usually feels shame or questions their faith on whether to remarry.

With divorce there can be concerns about decisions to divorce and remarry, as well as about the stigma that comes with both. Is divorce a decision? Yes—and no. Divorce is a decision but may not always be one made by both partners. One partner may find that his or her spouse has quit the marriage leaving him or her no choice but to file or sign divorce papers. There can be thoughts of failure or giving up but at the end most people getting divorced believe the decision was right and that ending the marriage was the best thing to do. The spouse can make the decision to not sign the divorce decree but that doesn't undo the fact that he or she is now single again. Then there are situations in which the marriage has crumbled to the point where both partners have decided it is time to end it.

Whether someone makes the decision to divorce or finds himself or herself single again without being part of the decision-making process, faith may play a huge role in how a person will feel during the process.

Divorce and Sin

People with faith believe they have made a covenant or contract and were united in marriage as one under the eyes of God. Divorce is the opposite of marriage—the process of taking what God has united as one and separating it into two once more—so it goes directly against the faith of many and therefore not only may be stigmatized but considered sinful. Those with the view that the act of divorce is a sin may separate themselves from the divorcee or shun him or her altogether.

Faith supports marriage but doesn't always support remarriage to a new partner in the case of divorce. In some situations, the thought of remarrying someone other than the previous spouse is often considered a sin. There are others who will look past the divorce and act to provide love and mercy for the people involved. In these situations, people in the church may still believe that divorce and remarrying is a sin, but they choose to treat people with love and support.

The culture today is more open and aware to the fact that a large number of marriages will break down and end in separation and divorce. Though today's culture is more open to divorce, based on one's faith divorce can still be very difficult for some people because they wonder about what members of their religion may say or how they will react. Also those experiencing divorce may feel that they have let God down.

Even today, unlike with death, there can be a stigma involved with divorce. Stigma is defined as "a mark of disgrace associated with a particular circumstance, quality, or person." The stigma may be something that someone feels or experiences through the actions of others and typically seems to be more present in faith circles than secular circles. Divorcees, whether or not they remarry, may find themselves ostracized in some social circles including their church communities.

To someone who has a strong spiritual belief, divorce can be devastating and confusing.

Christianity and Divorce

Christian churches do not advocate divorce, but most churches accept that marriages break down and are willing to recognize a civil divorce as valid to end the marriage, allowing a person to once again have a church wedding with someone other than his or her former partner.

There are other churches which take a negative view of divorce based on the teachings of Jesus on divorce in the New Testament where divorce can be viewed as adultery: *"I tell you that anyone who divorces his wife, except for sexual immorality, and marries another woman commits adultery."* (Matthew 19:9 NIV). Different Christian churches interpret this passage in different ways. Some view that a divorcee remarrying someone new isn't committing a sin if both partners are professing Christians; others do not.

Jane was raised in a very strict Protestant denominational church that believed that divorce was a sin. She was afraid that she wouldn't be forgiven for divorcing her ex-husband and moving in with her new husband before they were married. Even though she wasn't practicing her faith nor going to church, the lessons she had been taught as a child and a teenager caused her to have guilt. Her biggest fear was that the people of her faith who believed divorce was a sin, including her family member and friends, would judge her and look down on her because she had chosen to divorce her husband and remarry someone new.

She finally told her family and at first, they fought to accept her divorce since they were very religious and had the belief that marriage was for life. Her mother was the last to accept the divorce since she was old fashioned in her thinking and believed that a woman should wait until her husband changed. Her mother still struggled with the divorce until Jane opened up and shared the pains of her marriage that she had kept hidden.

Jane explained to her mother how, when Matt wasn't working on his job, he spent all of his free time hanging out with his buddies. His actions made her feel like she was second in his life and not number one. His treatment of her caused her to develop an unhealthy low self-esteem where she was depressed to the point that she felt alone even when she and Matt were physically together. She had done all she could to save her marriage, she had even joined a gym and stuck to a stringent diet to make herself more attractive and appealing to her husband. That had not helped, and Jane told her mom that she needed to get out of the marriage for the benefit of her mental, emotional and spiritual health.

If Jane had lost her husband through death, she would have had no feelings of guilt and shame, nor would she have worried about being judged for her decision to remarry. She would have possibly experienced the pain of losing the one she used to love but Jane would have felt God's acceptance and the support of her church community. Instead she had to deal with those feelings and her doubts about whether God and the church would forgive her for her divorce.

Annulment

While the Protestant faith allows divorce, the Catholic Church forbids it unless the marriage is first terminated by an annulment or through the death of a spouse.

Should one of the partners choose to remarry a new mate and have a new wedding ceremony in the Catholic Church, he or she will need to file an annulment declaring the previous marriage invalid, and that annulment will have to be reviewed and decided upon by a Church Tribunal after the person is counseled by a deacon or priest. The annulment will officially terminate a person's marriage in the eyes of the church and God. Without an annulment, a couple can be legally divorced based on civil law, but the Catholic Church will not recognize the civil divorce and will still consider the couple married in the "eyes of God," which means the divorcee will be considered living in sin and is not supposed to receive Holy

Communion.

Joe was a very faithful Catholic and decided to get an annulment through the church after his divorce. He decided on the annulment process because he felt that his marriage had not been a real marriage as his faith would describe it. The annulment process required that three additional people besides Joe complete a questionnaire that consisted of twenty-one questions.

It included questions such as "What should marriage look like?" "Is there spiritual hope?" "Was this marriage really a marriage in the eyes of God?" "What does it mean to have a faith-based marriage?" Joe's wife chose not to be part of the annulment process but did ask to see a copy of the questions. She was very hurt when she saw his answers since she and Joe had produced two beautiful children from their marriage that "never occurred." Joe felt bad that his ex-wife had been hurt by the questions, but the annulment was something that he felt strongly about and he wanted to stay faithful to the Church and be able to receive Holy Communion again.

Islam and Divorce

Divorce is not encouraged but is allowed in Islam because Muslims recognize that marriages often break down in today's society. When faced with marital conflict, the couple is encouraged to seek reconciliation by enlisting at least one family member from each of their families or seeking mediation from a family counselor or therapist to provide mediation. The mediation is to help the couple overlook the faults of each other. If it fails, as a last resort the couple will proceed with the divorce. Faith is very important and serves as a guiding light–since the couple signed a contract to marry, they must now break the contract to divorce.

Islam contains a set of divorce and remarriage procedures should a divorcee desire to remarry. The methods of Muslim divorce vary based on faith and gender and do not need to occur in a Mosque. The civil divorce will satisfy state law but doesn't satisfy the requirements of the Muslim faith which requires a religious divorce, an Islamic divorce that is recognized by the Islamic Sharia Council.

When a Muslim man initiates a divorce or "talaq," the process will differ based on whether he is Sunni or Shi'ah. A Sunni Muslim man will not need witnesses, where the Shi`ah Muslim man will need two witnesses when declaring the desire for divorce. This declaration doesn't need to take place in a Mosque, but the husband must announce on three separate occasions that he wants a divorce.

There is a three-month waiting period (three menstrual cycles) known as an "iddah" to ensure that the woman is not pregnant before the divorce is allowed. This waiting period serves as a time where the husband can decide that he doesn't want a divorce. If during this time it is discovered that the wife is pregnant, this is considered another opportunity to reconcile, but reconciliation is not required and she is free to divorce her husband. Once final, then both the man and woman are free to remarry.

A Muslim wife desiring a divorce will need to initiate the divorce proceedings known as the "Khul`a" or Marriage Dissolution. The woman doesn't need the permission of her husband to initiate the divorce. She will complete the Khul`a application and submit it to the council. Her husband is then notified that his wife has initiated the divorce. He can choose to not divorce but Islamic law does not prohibit her from still getting one. Once the husband consents to divorce and signs the agreement then an Islamic divorce certificate will be issued.

Saima Mir recounts the stigma she felt by her own divorce in her Feb. 16, 2019 article, "Divorce, Islam and me: 'I will forever be the woman who left two husbands'" printed in the British newspaper, *The Guardian*. Divorce is not uncommon in the Muslim faith and remarriage to a new love is not an issue, however there is a stigma that a woman faces after divorce. Saima said:

"I was lucky to have parents who trusted my judgment and didn't care what other people had to say. And people did have a lot to say. Divorce may be perfectly allowable according to

Islam (the Prophet's first wife was a divorcee), but that didn't stop the gossip. In a society that prizes virginity, my 'value' had fallen.

"The easiest way for a woman to regain her status after a divorce is to say her husband was impotent. It would have been easy to say I was still a virgin, but that would have been a lie. The truth was simple. I had been married and I was now divorced. And though I knew there was nothing wrong with my decision, my relatives' condolences left me feeling dirty, as if I had been the victim of a sex crime. I remember scrubbing myself in the shower until I almost bled, trying to clean away my shame."

There would have been no stigma experienced by Saima if she had lost her husband through death. In death, there would have been folks supporting her return to single life instead of gossiping about her situation. She would not have felt isolated from society but would have felt included.

Judaism and Divorce

Many Jewish couples who are having marital problems will try to sort them out. However, sometimes a couple might feel that their only option is divorce. Divorce in Jewish culture is viewed as something that sometimes happens in today's society and is viewed with sadness, but Jewish law doesn't forbid it or see it as a sinful act.

A civil divorce filed through the state may be legal and binding, but it will not satisfy Jewish law. Depending on how observant a couple is of Jewish law, the couple will follow the teachings of the Torah that "demands absolutely and unequivocally that marriage be terminated by formal religious divorce, or a *get*," author Maurice Lamm says in his book. The *get* is a Jewish bill of divorce that is based on Deuteronomy 24:1 (NIV) where the husband "writes her a certificate of divorce, gives it to her and sends her from his house." The husband and wife meet together at the rabbi's office where a scribe will complete the *get*, a document containing twelve lines of text that is then signed by two witnesses. Once signed, the husband will then present the *get* to his wife officially terminating the divorce according to Jewish law and freeing each to marry a new mate. Without the *get* the woman cannot remarry according to the teachings of traditional Jewish law. A Jewish believer that identifies with the liberal Jewish Reform movement may be satisfied with the civil divorce process for ending the marriage. However, should you wish to remarry a new mate in a Jewish ceremony, neither conservative nor orthodox rabbis will perform the ceremony if you do not have proof of divorce under Jewish law; a *get* assures that any future marriage is recognized by all sects of Judaism.

However, if the couple identifies with the Orthodox movement then they will adhere to the traditional teaching of Jewish law and the husband will need to give his wife a *get*. "Only a Jewish divorce ends a Jewish marriage. Only a Jewish divorce permits remarriage," Lamm says.

Without the *get* the couple is not considered divorced in the eyes of God even if they have a finalized civil divorce decree. The husband has an option to refuse his wife, but the practice is frowned upon in the Jewish community and the husband can be excommunicated from the synagogue. Without the *get* a woman who remarries will be considered "Agunah," meaning she is still married by Jewish law and may not remarry. If she remarries a new husband it will be seen as an act of adultery and any children born to the new couple would be viewed as illegitimate. A rabbi may not agree to officiate a Jewish ceremony without a Jewish divorce because the woman will still be considered married in the eyes of Jewish law.

Prior to marriage, Sarah didn't adhere to strict Orthodox Jewish law traditions and instead followed the Reform Judaism views which were more liberal than Jewish traditions. When Sarah married her husband David, he followed the Orthodox Jewish traditions and she chose to adopt his Orthodox views advocating strict observance of Jewish Law. During their marriage, they were able to create two beautiful children, a son and a daughter and worked together to raise their children under the teachings of Orthodox Jewish traditions. They were a happy couple until their marriage deteriorated, ending in divorce.

Sarah filed for divorce at her local courthouse to legally terminate their marriage which satisfied the legal requirements of her state but didn't satisfy Jewish law. Under Jewish law she and David were still considered married and were required to complete a *get* to satisfy Jewish law. To initiate the process, Sarah requested a *get* from David and they met in their rabbi's office where David provided Sarah with the Jewish divorce document. Once Sarah accepted, they were officially divorced according to Jewish law. Without the *get* she would have been considered Agunah and no rabbi would agree to officiate a Jewish wedding. And should she remarry, any children born to her and her new mate would be considered illegitimate under Jewish law because she would still be married in the eyes of God.

Conclusion

If faith plays a major role in someone's marriage, then it will also play a huge role in how someone responds to the death of a loved one or the death of dream through divorce. Depending on a person's religious faith, there can be different reactions between becoming single from the death of a loved one and through the act of divorce. Losing someone through death does not provoke accusations of sin and wrongful doing—unless the surviving spouse had a hand in the death of the spouse.

Likewise, when someone loses someone through death there is an expectation that members of his or her religious group will provide support—but this isn't always the case with divorce. Whether one's faith is Christian, Jewish, or Islam, divorce will provoke different reactions from their respective religious communities. Many a divorcee can immediately incur accusations of sin even if the partner had no choice because his or her spouse walked out.

Remarriage can also result in accusations of sin should a divorcee decide to remarry someone other than his or her former spouse. Support from a person's religious group can also still vary even though divorce occurs more often in today's society. There will be those who will make divorcees feel loved and supported while others will stigmatize and even ostracize them.

The best metaphor that I have yet to read is from the article, "The Jewish View of Divorce - divorce is a tragedy, but sometimes it's the right thing to do" by Aron Moss on the Jewish website Chabad.org. Moss likened divorce to the amputation of a limb, such as an arm or leg, that has become diseased. The limb is part of the body and must be cut off or the body will most likely eventually die. Just like no one wants to have to make a decision to amputate a limb, no one wants to have to decide to divorce. When faced with a life or death situation, however, the decision to amputate is difficult but must be made to save the person's life; the same is often true with divorce.

In hindsight Jane feels that her faith prolonged the inevitable and she stayed in her marriage longer than she should have because she believed, according to her faith, that she should not get divorced. However, she finally had to make a choice to divorce when staying in the marriage was more painful than the thought that her action would be a sin. Even though she wasn't practicing her faith during and after the divorce, the sinful weight of her decision was heavy…but the alternative was too much to bear.

When Jane decided to divorce, she eventually sought out a loving church where she was able to receive support and find solace in her faith. Her new church didn't judge her decision to leave her husband and she found that they provided her emotional support during and after her divorce. Even though many may have had views that divorce was wrong and should not have happened, they looked past her situation and looked at her as a person who was deserving of love and support which she so desperately needed during such a critical time.

"Peace I leave with you; my peace I give you. I do not give to you as the world gives. Do not let your hearts be troubled and do not be afraid." –John 14:27 (NIV)

CHAPTER 9: FUTURE

"Moving on doesn't mean you forget about things, it just means you have to accept what happened and continue living." –Erza Scarlet, Fictional character

As my parents went through their divorce, I witnessed first-hand many of the things discussed in the book, ranging from a broken heart to faith. I never thought much about a process for moving on when their divorce was finalized. There was no celebration of divorce where family members gathered; I remember it as a day that came and went without fanfare. It didn't feel like a chapter of my life was over, it felt like the whole book had just ended. I didn't know how or where to start in writing my new story, the one where my mom and dad were no longer married.

I thought that the moving on process for me merely meant that I needed to recognize *Life sucks! Man up! Move on!* I know that wasn't the approach that I should have taken, but I don't remember being aware of another process. I was a twenty-year-old boy, filled with rage, resentment and sadness.

When the divorce happened, I had no plan to move on, no process to grieve because no one ever taught me how. I only saw a bleak future ahead and tried to make it through each day. During the final days of the divorce I joined the United States Army in hopes to have a better future. It was a decision that I have never regretted because it put me in a new environment which helped me deal with the divorce. I was starting a new chapter in my life. But the real turning point for me was when I learned to focus on the only real hope, and that was God.

Four years after the divorce, I found a good church that helped me establish a way to rekindle and develop a relationship with Jesus Christ built on love and mercy. Without that guiding light I would not have been able to eventually overcome the pains of my parent's divorce nor face multiple other hardships I would come to experience throughout my life like we all do. Having that relationship has also helped my wife stay married to me for over thirty years.

Whether you're affected by your own divorce or that of a loved one as a child, parent, or other family member or friend, the goal of this chapter is to introduce you to some action steps to take to help you move on.

In anything, you must take action Friedman and James tell us in their book *Moving On*: "You cannot read your way into a successful relationship, but you can read and then take the actions that will lead you to a successful one."

Alexandra Kennedy states in her article, *"Healing a broken heart after the loss of a loved one"* (*Monterey Herald*, 2015) that "the key to healing a broken heart is to learn how to grieve fully without feeling overwhelmed."

Divorce is a traumatic, painful, and stressful event, whether it was straightforward or messy. Everyone needs to take time to heal, which means "to make well again: to restore to health," as defined by Merriam-Webster.

The Homes-Rahe Life Stress Inventory lists death of a spouse as the number one stressor in life out of the top one hundred with divorce, or death of a dream, as a close second.

The Do's
Take Time *and* Action to Grieve

Whether people feel they are the victims in a marriage and view their divorce as freeing, or believe they are the victims of a divorce because they had no choice in the matter, there needs to be a time for grieving. Either way the hopes, dreams, and aspirations planned for the marriage on the wedding day have just died.

Authors Friedman and James in *The Grief Recovery Handbook* suggest that after a traumatic event, a person lives in "the deception of academy award recovery" for their acting skills in pretending that they are doing well. But it's ok to not be ok.

Donna recounted that, "The day that I signed my divorce papers is a day I will never forget because after I signed them, making my divorce final, I broke down and cried." As someone takes time to grieve the death of a loved one, please take time to grieve the death of a dream. There is grief recovery available.

Seek Therapy

Take action and seek therapy. Remember there is no medical device available that will provide a visual picture of a broken heart, but therapy treatment does provide an opportunity to get an independent assessment of what you may be feeling and confirm if there are legitimate concerns.

Contact a leader of your faith or a medical professional to find a certified therapist who has been trained to ask questions and communicate in a way to help draw out and recognize issues you may have of which you are unaware, and to assist you with working through them. Be aware that the first therapist you contact may not be the best fit; just like you would search for and find the right doctor when you're dealing with a physical aliment, you may need to seek a second opinion.

Seeking therapy doesn't mean that you are weak but echoes how strong and smart you are for recognizing that pain exists in order to get an independent assessment from a medical professional. If you had experienced a break in your arm wouldn't you want to seek the advice of a doctor to examine your arm? It's natural for someone to seek counseling after the death of a loved one so therefore it is natural for someone to seek it after the death of a dream.

Focus on Personal Growth

When actor Dennis Quaid got divorced he aptly said, "when you break up, your whole identity is shattered. That's why it's like death. It is a death."

Take time to discover who you are. In her article, "After Divorce: 8 Tips for Reinventing Yourself" from WebMD, 2012, Gina Shaw suggests that you should take time to "rediscover who you used to be" before you were married. When you and your spouse became a couple, there may have been people, places or things that you gave up or quit doing. Take a moment and ask the question, "Who am I?" Embrace being single and don't mistake being alone as loneliness but appreciate your solitude and enjoy being alone.

Natalie had just ended a fifteen-year relationship with Vince and remarked that one of the first things she needed to do was rediscover who she was. She didn't realize how much she had adapted to accommodate her ex until the relationship ended. She was sad that the relationship was over, but she rediscovered the things in life that she had enjoyed prior to meeting Vince and realized that once she had met him, she had slowly drifted away from herself to become part of him.

Suddenly Natalie was sitting alone one Saturday morning wondering what to do with the day that stretched out before her. In her previous single life, she recalled weekend afternoons when she had enjoyed gardening, long hikes and creative cooking, trying new recipes with fresh vegetables from her garden. She remembered hanging out with old friends. When she was with Vince she had spent all of her time with him and didn't have time to catch up with friends.

Natalie decided it was time to reclaim the activities she had so enjoyed—and it would start today. She began the day with a long walk, then went to the local landscaping store to buy some gardening tools and plants. She enjoyed gardening and living in a condo didn't stop her. She and her friend Tina took advantage of the community garden and rented a space to scratch their gardening itch. Eventually she began meeting Tina to harvest fresh vegetables from the garden. One day they returned to Natalie's condo and cooked a delicious vegetable lasagna which they enjoyed while sitting on Natalie's balcony jotting down the names of friends to invite to a "celebration of Natalie" party.

You may not be like Natalie and have spare time to yourself but instead you find yourself as the sole caregiver for your young children while working a full-time job. There may seem like there is no time to rediscover who you were prior to marriage. Still, this is a time for you to reinvent the new you. Aristotle said, "Knowing yourself is the beginning of all wisdom." When you ask "Who am I?" the answer may come back that you are a single parent whose life revolves around your children and when you aren't with the kids, you are working full-time providing for their well-being. That's who you are right now and that's ok—you still want to make the best of it, live life to the fullest and enjoy yourself.

Tracy discovered that once the divorce was over she didn't have time to rediscover herself and who she had been prior to marriage and had to reinvent herself. She was now a single mom, working full-time and her life now revolved around her kids.

Even though this was hard, she appreciated this new life and time with her children because she eventually realized that any time she spent with her kids was a limited time offer that came with an expiration date—they would grow up soon enough.

Tracy had five children, four daughters and a son. Funds were more limited after her divorce so she was restricted somewhat with the activities they could do, but she was willing to work extra hours at her job to earn money so her kids could enjoy themselves. She managed her days so she could spend more time with the kids. They had picnics in the park and cookouts with their grandparents, aunts, uncles and cousins. She would buy the family a season pass to Six Flags America so she and the kids could spend the summer building memories on the roller coasters, which the kids loved (and Tracy tolerated.) If that was not enough, she wanted to give the kids something special so she also purchased family season passes to Busch Gardens and Water Country USA.

Get Help for Your Kids

Author and mom Anna Quindlen says, "Your children make it impossible to regret your past. They're its finest fruits. Sometimes the only ones."

Be sure to help children move on as well as yourself. If you have children from your previous marriage then the divorce process can be more difficult than if you're single; you and your former partner have created a permanent link between the both of you that will continue until you're gone.

In some cases, depending on their ages and the situation itself, the children may have been aware of mom and dad having problems but never imagined divorce and may be experiencing some shock. Please take time to sit down with your children and have a conversation about the divorce and what it means to them and for their lives. Remember their lives have been uprooted and disrupted from the divorce and they have experienced their own loss.

"Divorce isn't the child's fault. Don't say anything unkind about your ex to the child, because you're really just hurting the child," says actress Valerie Bertinelli, who got divorced in 2007. Bertinelli, of "One Day at a Time" TV show fame, was married for over twenty years to Eddie Van Halen, member and founder of the rock group Van Halen. Most of their marriage was rocky, but one shining star came from their marriage—their son Wolfgang. When Valerie was on the Oprah Show in 2008 she made the following comment: "One of the many reasons that Ed and I split up is to give Wolfie a better vision of what two people who are supposedly in love treat each other like. Ed and I weren't treating each other like two people that loved each other, and that's what Wolfie was seeing," she said. "So I'm hoping that when he does get married and start a life for himself, that he takes his time and marries a friend and not just someone that he can't keep his hands off."

Remember kids will normally love both parents and will

have developed their own special, unique bonds with each parent that are different than those that the parents had with each other. Even though the parents may have grown apart and may at times even develop a hateful relationship with each other, the child will love both parents and it can be very hurtful to be put "in the middle"—to hear parents degrade or bad mouth each other.

One thing I really admired about my mother when she and my dad divorced is that she never "trash-talked" my dad or said anything negative about him to me and my brothers. Thankfully, my dad reciprocated.

Children may be confused as to why their parents chose to divorce. In many cases there are plenty of grounds for divorce...perhaps it was based on physical or mental abuse making it easy to understand why the marriage ended. However, in some cases, such as when one parent just got tired of being married or chose another partner and decided to end the marriage, the children may be left baffled, wondering why their parents are splitting up.

The parents may tell their children that mom and dad are unhappy, but that is hard for kids to understand. The children may reason with themselves that they are happy and don't see a problem. In some cases, they blame themselves.

Liam was eleven-years old and had just returned home from school after being dropped at his house by the school bus. When he came into the house, his mother asked him to sit down next to her on their living room couch, took his hand, looked into his eyes and broke the news that she and his dad were divorcing. Liam was shocked to hear the news. He was also frustrated and didn't understand why his parents were divorcing. He had a good relationship with his father. Even though his dad was gone often, Liam still had a great time when they were together. They would spend many weekend afternoons tossing the football around in the backyard and taking fishing trips together. The relationship might not always have been close but it was a positive relationship. Liam was happy.

Now Liam began to feel like he was responsible for the divorce. After the divorce was final, Liam's father started to distance himself from his son. Liam no longer saw his father and he really missed his relationship with his dad. Liam chose to blame his mother and he began to have problems in school where he struggled with anger and behavioral problems.

Fortunately, Liam's mother didn't dismiss his concerns but recognized his feelings and spent time helping him to resolve his anger and behavior problems and to understand the reason for the divorce, reinforcing that he was not responsible. While Liam's grades suffered for a little while, they did eventually spike back up and he was able to focus once again, becoming the fun-loving kid he was before, spending his free time playing baseball with his friends.

If his mother hadn't listened and spent time helping him, Liam would have likely dropped off the baseball team and maybe even failed out of school instead.

It is also very important to remember that each child has his or her own personality and may react differently than their siblings. Don't make the mistake of asking a son or daughter, "Why can't you be like your brother or sister?" Children are not their brothers or sisters, they are unique human beings with their own DNA codes.

Gail discovered that fact with her two daughters. Her oldest daughter seemed to handle the divorce very well, but her younger child did not and started to overeat. She eventually gained fifty pounds over the period of twelve months when she was in seventh grade—a critical time when she was bullied for being overweight, which drastically affected her self-esteem. Gail found therapy for her younger daughter. Coming to realize that each of her daughters was unique helped her understand that one daughter wasn't stronger or weaker, they were each just different and needed individual help through the divorce.

A word of caution...do not use your kids as a substitute for your own therapist by dumping your adult problems, pains, and concerns onto their backs. They have plenty of kid problems that they are dealing with as well.

Carlton realized that his wife started using their two teenaged daughters for therapy by treating them as adult peers and began sharing her problems with them. He recognized that this interaction was having a negative effect on his daughters and reached out to their school counselor to get a recommendation for a psychiatrist, psychologist or therapist for them to see. Carlton reasoned that if his child had an earache, he would try and find her the best help possible to cure it. Instead of an earache, his daughters were dealing with a broken heart and too much pressure from their mom.

He found a therapist and began sending his children to her. She in turn provided him with an independent assessment. The counselor also provided the daughters with someone with whom to discuss topics that they were not comfortable talking about with their dad. It took two years but the therapy paid huge dividends in his daughters' well-being.

Get Help from Family

"I sustain myself with the love of family." –Maya Angelou, Author

Hopefully you're fortunate enough to be able to seek out family members who can be supportive and assist you as you transition to your newfound life. This shift in your life may have been something you chose, or the change may be one that was forced upon you. Loving family members can come to your aid and serve as a support team to help make you feel that you are not alone in this next phase of your life.

Until you are established in your new role, family members may be able to assist in providing children with transportation to and from school or maybe running errands as you transition to your new life. This can be an overwhelming time where a new single parent experiences growing pains and stress and will greatly appreciate family members providing them with moments of quiet time and solitude so they can take a deep breath and refocus.

If needed, loving family members can assist you with

financial help or temporary living arrangements providing you time to find adequate and affordable housing.

Tammy's family helped her and her daughter when her husband suddenly walked out on the family. Tammy was barely getting by with a minimum wage job as a waitress at a local diner and was unable to continue to pay the rent on their home, so they were forced to move out. She reached out to her parents who not only provided her with shelter and financial aid to help her pay her bills, but also provided loving emotional support for her and their granddaughter. This reprieve from having to find immediate shelter provided Tammy with the time to search and find affordable housing that accommodated her needs helping to make the change easier.

Family can be supportive when you may have doubts on whether you made the best decision or believe that you didn't try hard enough and feel like a failure.

Harry had concerns when it came time to tell his family that he was having problems in his marriage of eight years. He finally found the courage to make the call to his mother and tell her that he and his wife were getting a divorce. Her response was uplifting when she told her son that she had concerns for years about his marriage to her daughter-in-law. She was quick to tell him that she supported his decision, which helped him mentally and emotionally in going through the process. Sometimes the folks nearest you realize that your marriage is over years before you do and wonder what took you so long to make the decision to divorce.

Get Help from Friends

"One who has unreliable friends soon comes to ruin, but there is a friend who sticks closer than a brother." Proverbs 18:24 (NIV)

You may lose friends during the breakup, so it is essential to seek out a core set of friends to call your own during and after the divorce. "A real friend is one who walks in when the rest of the world walks out," advised the late U.S. journalist Walter Winchell.

Having a core group of trusted friends, or at least one good one to talk to after the breakup of a marriage, is important to the emotional state and recovery of someone getting divorced. A trusted friend can help fill a void left by the ex. Surround yourself with friends you trust who can be your confidantes, allowing you to share and vent without worrying that your words will get back to your ex, a family member, or other friends. Friends can often give a different perspective on the breakup providing an objective viewpoint free of fear and anger.

There is a Russian proverb, "It's better to be slapped by the truth than kissed with a lie." Be careful accepting feedback from well-meaning friends who may choose to kiss you with a lie so they don't have to provide negative feedback that may hurt your feelings. Seek out friends who are willing to slap you in the face with the truth by telling you about your role in causing the divorce. Many people want to surround themselves with people who will only tell them how messed up the ex was or how great they were, but to move on everyone needs to acknowledge their own role so they can see the areas where they need to change. The only person we can ever change is ourselves of course.

Coming clean about your own part in the divorce and the role that you possibly played in the breakup whether major or minor will help you see improvements that you can make and create good habits that you can take into your next relationship.

Gail was able to rebound from the break-up of her marriage by engaging her girlfriends to help her during this period. She had confided in her girlfriends during the divorce process so they were available to help console her during and after and were a pivotal part in helping her get through it. She was able to fill the void of companionship by making it a priority to schedule time with her girlfriends by spending evenings and downtime to help her move on. And they helped her see her part in the breakup so she could eventually find a new husband and have a healthier marriage with him in the future.

I've heard it said that "your absolute best won't ever be good enough for the wrong people. At your worst, you'll still be worth it to the right ones." During the marriage, Gail had worked hard at being a good wife to her husband. She had worked a full-time job, and in the evenings, she ensured that dinner was ready and her family was well cared for. When her divorce was final, she kept asking what she could have done differently to save her marriage. While on a girls night out with some of her friends they helped her see what she couldn't see: that she needed to stop settling and trying to adapt to someone else's approval, that she needed to stop being a people-pleaser because nothing she ever did was good enough.

It was necessary for Gail to step back and define how she wanted to be treated and what compatibility really meant for her. She had to accept the fact that the only person that she could change was herself, not anyone else. She learned that if she carried the same old her into her bright new future, then she would only dim it. She had to bring a new Gail if she wanted to have a good relationship with a new husband.

The lack of trusted friends during and after a divorce can inhibit a person's growth needed to help him or her move on. It may also cause that person to seek out substitutes that will fill the void that friends should fill. Alcohol or substance abuse, gambling and work overload are just a few unhealthy activities divorcees might engage in if they're not surrounded by good friends.

Jack was someone who didn't have any close male friends during his marriage which made it hard for him to surround himself with any after his divorce. He spent most of his free time in a bar drinking beer to fill the void and serve as his therapy sessions, which made it difficult for him to recover and move on after his divorce.

Seek Follow-up Legal Help

"Have a final follow-up meeting with your divorce lawyer" advises Senior Lifestyle Reporter Brittany Wong.

You are probably at a point where you are just glad the divorce is finished. However, as you try to move on afterward, the legal aftermaths can continue to pop up for years. If you used legal counsel during your divorce, then schedule a meeting with your lawyer after the divorce is finalized. In the article, "The First Thing You Must Do When Your Divorce Is Final" by Brittany Wong (Huffpost, 2017), during that meeting take time to learn about legal issues that may pop up in the future which may require you to go back to court. Work with your lawyer to understand and learn about issues that could occur in the future and what you should do. Your lawyer can help you manage expectations and develop a strategy on how to handle various issues prior to a problem occurring.

Having the knowledge of an experienced lawyer and a legal strategy for the future will help you move on. A divorce lawyer is experienced with dealing with the legal aftermath of a divorce and the legal issues that can pop up post-divorce, and he or she can prepare you for possible issues that may arise. Working with the lawyer is especially important if this is your first divorce because you're not equipped with the knowledge and scenarios that your lawyer has witnessed or familiar with what can happen.

Get Your Finances in Order

"The worry over money was one of the worst things about my divorce," says Leah Williams (fictional name of real woman interviewed)

You are single again. Take a moment to square away your finances because money can be a sincere concern and cause stress making it difficult to move on. If you were already handling the family finances, then you will have knowledge of your income and expenses. However, if you weren't responsible for any of the family bills then you will need to develop an understanding of your current finances and responsibilities. Develop a budget consisting of your new income including spousal support, and your expenditures such as utilities, rent or mortgage, car payments, and credit card debt to provide you an overall view of your financial situation. Will you need to find employment or a second job to help support yourself or will existing financial support be sufficient?

After reviewing her financial situation, Leah and her children had to move to a different more affordable house that they rented instead of owned in a different part of the same town so her kids could attend the same schools. She worked one full-time job, but also took on a part-time job working every day, so she was working about fifty-five hours a week to support her family. Leah did what she had to do to preserve her family's lifestyle as much as possible so as not to add any more disruptions or changes to the chaos that had already occurred due to the divorce.

Review any savings accounts, existing loans, and credit cards to get a complete list of the accounts where you and your ex are both listed as joint owners or borrowers. Where possible have your name removed from the accounts, credit cards and loans or ensure that your name is only on accounts where you are the sole owner or borrower. Make sure your name is only on accounts that you are responsible for because if you and your ex are both listed as joint owners and if your ex should default and not make the payments, the creditors will contact you for payment.

Take a moment to review your company pension plans and life insurance and health insurance policies to ensure they are current with your new status. Be sure to update the beneficiary information now that you are no longer married. Medical insurance is very important to review since many times one spouse has a policy that covers the family. Review the policy with the ex to understand who will cover the children. Of course with the divorce, if the medical insurance was purchased by your ex-spouse then you will need to purchase a policy to cover you.

Tatyana Bunich of Financial 1 Wealth Management Group provides additional financial guidance for anyone who is divorcing later in life and has grown children: Work with a financial advisor to help you "bullet proof" your estate to protect your children's inheritance by ensuring they are the beneficiaries since that supersedes your will. In addition, should you remarry, it is recommended that you and your new mate sign a prenuptial agreement at the beginning outlining what assets each are bringing into the marriage.

Martin and Mary were both on their second marriage, each with children from their previous marriages, but didn't sign a prenuptial even though Mary brought a large estate into the marriage and Martin didn't. Mary and Martin had both worked together to build their own separate estate, with Mary never having to dip into the funds that she brought into the marriage.

Now years later they are working on their will and Mary wants to leave the estate that she brought into the marriage to her children and exclude her stepchildren. There is nothing malicious and Mary cares for her stepchildren, but her estate was something that she had worked to provide for her children. This was a bit contentious, but the couple worked out the issue with Mary consenting and including the stepchildren. This would not have been a problem if the discussion had happened at the beginning of their marriage.

Keep Your Faith
"But God is my helper. The Lord keeps me alive!" —Psalm 54:4 (NLT)

How observant people are of their faith will determine how much it will pertain in the moving-on process. For many folks, faith helps during good and bad times and may guide them in the decision-making process with divorce, and also affect them in the aftermath.

According to Jane Smith (fictional name of real woman interviewed), "the struggles and pain that are experienced with divorce are like no other, so find a church with loving people that will accept you as you are and not judge you for your decision to divorce."

Some, of course, may be faced with a stigma from members of their faith because the marriage didn't last.

Sarah felt the stigma of being a newly divorced woman but no stigma was placed on her husband since he was well-liked in the community. She accepted that there would be those in her synagogue who would judge her but their view of her didn't define who she was. Sarah switched synagogues while her ex stayed put but she was ok with that since her happiness was more important than having to drive an additional half hour to get to synagogue.

Not everyone will agree with you. Jesus Christ had twelve disciples or best friends and one of his best friends didn't agree with Him; you're not going to get a hundred percent agreement even if you can walk on water.

Jane was a very spiritual person and her relationship with God was most important—she believed that He hates divorce. Therefore, the hardest thing for her was dealing with the guilt and the belief that she wasn't close to God after her divorce, which made her feel as if she had drifted away from Him.

Those whose faith is the most important thing to them suffer greatly when they live in such a way they know God does not approve. It took several years after her divorce for Jane to feel like God and she were friends again. Her faith has grown exponentially since the divorce and even though it has been a difficult time in her life, it has also been a time of great peace and reliance on God's love and strength. For Jane it wasn't a choice of passive resignation but an active trusting in the goodness and power of God.

The Don't Dos

According to Allison James in her blog article, "3 Things You Shouldn't Do When Grieving a Divorce," (The Grief Recovery Method, 2015) there are three "don't dos" when grieving divorce. James stresses that "the key to recovery from grief is action not time."

The first is don't try and justify why you shouldn't be grieving by believing that you had a good reason for getting divorced and this is the best thing for you.

Second, you shouldn't pretend that the split shouldn't hurt when well-meaning friends are telling you to move on. It's ok if it hurts.

The third thing is not to immediately replace your lost spouse with someone else; your ex-partner wasn't a pair of old socks that can be switched out with a new pair.

Here is a "don't do" tip for family members and friends: Please err on the side of caution and don't attempt to console someone who has gone through a divorce by telling him or her that "this is the best decision you could make" or "you're better off without your ex," no matter how happy he or she may seem.

Mary said that she hated it when someone told her that she was "better off" after her divorce was finalized. She likened it to when a family member dies and people tell you he or she is "in a better place." Mary didn't consider her lost husband in a better place...a better place would be sitting next to her.

Conclusion

To ensure a safe and pleasant flight there are steps that need to be followed on an airplane before it arrives safely at its destination. One of the first steps passengers should take before boarding is to check their luggage and remove any excess baggage or weight so that they can board with a lighter load. Sometimes they just need to bring their carry-on luggage.

A similar baggage check-in process is needed for moving on after a divorce. Work with a therapist to help you "check-in" and leave behind the bulky, excess emotional baggage you don't need to take with you going forward. Take action to lighten your load and only bring your "carry-on luggage" with you—only that which you absolutely need for your bright new future.

Once aboard the plane the passengers take their seats. Before the plane can leave the ground, the flight attendants will review the safety features of the aircraft with the passengers. Each passenger has the responsibility for executing the steps such as the use of the oxygen mask. If the plane loses cabin pressure an oxygen mask will drop from the overhead compartment. Adult passengers need to ensure that they put their own oxygen masks on before placing masks on their accompanying children. Parents can't help their kids through the divorce process if they aren't already taking care of themselves first.

It is now time for takeoff...for you to start the next phase of your life. Keep in mind that no matter how prepared you are for a flight, the trip can sometimes be bumpy and require patience. Divorce is similar; no matter how you prepare to move on there will still be uncomfortable moments before you reach your destination. But keep the end in sight—your destination will be one of rebirth, a new you.

Have a safe flight!

AFTERWORD

"Any home can be a castle when the king and queen are in love." (Anonymous)

The king and queen start out with the happiest day of their lives—a day when they both vow their devoted love to each other. Years later the royal couple are enjoying life together in their castle until one of them utters the words, "I don't love you anymore," or "I have found someone else."

Just because one partner stops loving, it doesn't mean that the other partner stops loving back. Love is not a stream of water flowing through a spigot that can be turned on or off at a moment's notice. The partner receiving the bad news can't just push a button and stop loving his or her soulmate for life. You can't simply erase a familiar, oft-told story from your heart and mind when the last chapter ends and the book is closed.

Still, the fairytale is over, finished. The End.

The idea for this book was formed many years ago stemming from a conversation that still echoes in my ears. I was eighteen when I met my good friend Jill, an attractive thirty-something woman. She and I were sitting in my car outside her home. The sun was dropping below the horizon; the songbird chorus that wafted through the rolled-down windows was replaced by a symphony of grunting and croaking frogs. The night air became cool as she reminisced about her divorce and the aftershocks it created. She looked at me and in a serious tone said, "Stan, losing your spouse through divorce is worse than death. You see, in death you don't worry about seeing your best friend having dinner at your favorite restaurant with your ex-husband. That hurts!"

Just two years later, I learned firsthand the pains that divorce can bring when my parents divorced. Everyone dies, but not everyone gets divorced, especially not *my* parents. Their marriage wasn't violent, there was no abuse; they just became unhappy with each other.

The solution brought them happiness, but it broke my heart. My family as I knew it was shattered. I've had to bury both of my parents, and the pain and grief that I experienced with their deaths paled in comparison to the wound that their divorce sliced into all our lives.

Even with my parent's divorce I never understood the power of Jill's words, "divorce is worse than death" until one beautiful summer day about twenty years later while attending a friend's pool party with my wife. It was the beginning of summer and my wife and I were kicking off the season as a couple minus our daughters who were visiting friends enjoying some free time of their own away from mom and dad.

Everyone was enjoying the warmth of the sun, laughing with friends, feasting on burgers and hotdogs, washing it all down with their favorite beverages. I was balancing a paper plate that looked more like a backyard barbecue sampler tray, leaning in to catch the punchline of a joke over the shrill laugher from the teenagers doing cannonballs and splashing one another in the pool. I noticed that everyone was smiling, happy, except for one person—an old friend, a young woman named Heather.

I saw Heather standing there on the lawn, several feet from the pool's edge, dressed in a plain, somber gray covering of some sort, and I was surprised to see she wasn't wearing her characteristic smile that would usually light up a room. She seemed depressed, distracted and numb, not able to enjoy herself, so I approached her and asked her what was wrong. Blinking back tears, in a hesitant voice, she confided that she had recently divorced her husband. I looked in her eyes and with the same seriousness that Jill had used many years ago, I blurted out, "divorce is worse than death."

I told her that I understood...that I realized losing her husband through divorce was most likely worse than losing him in death, and it was ok to be sad and to grieve as if she were a widow. I will never forget how her countenance changed. She looked at me and instantly perked up. Her expression transformed from sadness to relief and her characteristic smile flickered like a candle in the darkness.

Other people had apparently been telling her that she needed to put her ex-husband behind her and start a new life. She was happy that the divorce was finally over, but she wasn't happy that the marriage was over. She had married him "until death do us part" but apparently her ex-husband had not been as committed. She still loved him. It was almost as if I gave her permission to grieve and she was relieved she no longer had to hide how she felt...and that she was no longer alone, that someone *understood.*

As I wrote this book, my mind kept drifting back to that summer pool party and how I was able to make a difference in the life of a dear friend who had experienced a divorce...just like Jill had done for me.

The purpose and hope of this book is that you, like me, will be able to make a positive difference in the life of a friend or family member who is going through or has gone through a painful, maybe even devastating, divorce or end of a relationship by listening, relating, understanding and giving them comfort and hope.

Death and divorce *are* different. Death is straightforward because *everyone dies.* Divorce, on the other hand, is complicated because *everyone does not get a divorce.*

The book wasn't written to discourage or encourage divorce but to help people who are going through it to realize that the process can feel as bad or even worse than death and in so doing, come to terms with it.

A local pastor reminded me that he had gone through some recent situations where he had lost a loved one, so he didn't entirely agree with the premise that divorce is worse than death. He is correct that divorce or death of a dream is not *always* worse than the death of a loved one, but for many people, the pain can be excruciating and worse than that experienced with a death.

In my research and interviews, I've learned that all divorces are unique. Each person has his or her own personal story to tell. Even if the divorce was based on mutual consent, there is still some sadness because the dreams and hopes that the couple had on their wedding day have perished.

But the good news is that life not only goes on but can get better after death *and* divorce. The moving on process may happen in phases, and it may take a few months or a few years for your life to turn around. But fairytales do happen.

From the GodUpdates website, writer Mel Johnson shares the true story, "A Mom Shares Her Story of Love After Divorce" of Kristina Kuzmic, a blogger mom who was able to find her fairytale.

Kristina experienced a difficult divorce that left her as a single mom of two young children, a son and a daughter. Her divorce left her cynical and not open to having another relationship. When she met Philip, she gave him every reason to stay away. But Kristina recognized that this new man in her life was unlike any other man she had ever met because no matter what she did, Philip saw the best in her. She finally invited Philip over to meet her son and daughter but was careful not to show any affection toward him so she wouldn't give her kids any reason to believe that he was anything other than just one of her friends.

Then the big night happened when she discovered Philip was her Prince Charming. Kristina reminisced:

"A few weeks after he met the kids, I had a particularly hard night. I was sick, and my 3-year-old woke up in the middle of the night throwing up all over the carpet, which, of course, woke my 5-year-old up, who screamed and cried in exhaustion. We were a mess, all three of us. It was one of those single-mom moments where I thought I would go insane. I looked insane, probably smelled insane, and my head was pounding from

all the screaming. I was trying to calm my children and clean up my daughter and the carpet, and I thought, 'Why would any man sign up for this?'

I called Philip and woke him up. 'Come over. Come over right now. You say you want me, you say you want my life with everything that comes along with it, then come over.'

He was at my apartment within 20 minutes. The kids were still screaming, and I was on all fours on the floor, scrubbing the carpet. I expected a look of shock or disgust, maybe even anger that I had woken him up in the middle of the night for this. But instead, without missing a beat, he got down on that floor, grabbed the rag out of my hand, sent me to bed, and cleaned up my daughter's vomit.

Then he tucked my children in and got them to sleep. And then he tucked me in, kissed my forehead, and said, 'Yes, I want this. I want every part of it. All three of you'."

Kristina met her Prince Charming and not only did he want her, but he was ready to embrace her whole kingdom, her little prince and princess, and the ups and downs that would come with a life together. It wasn't just a fairytale come true for Kristina, it was a fairytale come true for her children. She found a husband and the kids found a dad.

In her YouTube video titled "Don't Settle," Kristina tells more of her story about finding her "happily ever after" and gives everyone hope: "...I'm telling you right now there are still wonderful people out there who will genuinely love you and who will love your children as their own, and you deserve that..."

This is the end of the book but just the beginning for you. Your fairytale awaits!

BIBLIOGRAPHY

Foreword

American Psychological Association. n.d. "Understanding psychological testing and assessment." accessed April 4, 2020. https://www.apa.org/helpcenter/assessment

Independent Imaging. "The ABC's of Imaging: The Difference between XRay, UltraSound, MRI, CT Scan." February 15, 2018. https://www.independentimaging.com/abcs-imaging-difference-xray-ultrasound-mri-ct-scan/

Chapter 1: Grief

Comanche

Merriam-Webster. "Dictionary by Merriam-Webster: America's most-trusted online dictionary." Accessed April 2, 2020. http://www.merriam-webster.com/

Hauck, Kenneth. *A time to grieve: journeying through grief, book one.* Saint Louis: Stephen Ministries. 2004.

Stages of Grief

Kübler-Ross, Elisabeth. *On Death and Dying.* New York: Scribner Classics. 1997.

Burke, L.J. "Seven Stages of Grief During and After Divorce" *Divorce Magazine.* Updated January 7, 2020. https://www.divorcemag.com/articles/stages-of-grief-during-and-after-divorce

Westberg, Granger E. *Good Grief.* Minneapolis: Fortress Press. 2011.

Conclusion

Stephen Moeller, "Divorce and Grief," (blog), The Grief Recovery Method, February 9, 2017, https://www.griefrecoverymethod.com/blog/2017/02/divorce-and-grief

Chapter 2: Children

Custody Case Continues

Baskerville, Stephen. *Taken into custody: the war against fathers, marriage, and the family.* Nashville: Cumberland House. 2007.

Healthline. "What Is Parental Alienation Syndrome?" December 5, 2019. https://www.healthline.com/health/childrens-health/parental-alienation-syndrome

Cordano, Emy A. (blog) "Why Do Women Get Child Custody In 90 Percent Of All Cases? Isn't It Gender Discrimination?" Emy A Cordano. Updated July 24, 2019. https://www.cor-law.com/blog/women-get-child-custody-90-percent-cases-isnt-gender-discrimination.html

Chapter 3: Home

Keith, T. (1994). *Who's that man?* Nashville: PolyGram Records

Nemovitz, Bruce. (9 December 2019) "Selling Your Home: The 5 Stages of Loss and Grief." Laureate Group. December 9, 2019. https://www.laureategroup.com/blog/selling-your-home-the-5-stages-of-loss-and-grief/

What Makes a House a Home?

Merriam-Webster. "Dictionary by Merriam-Webster: America's most-trusted online dictionary." Accessed April 2, 2020. http://www.merriam-webster.com/

Who Should Keep the Home?

Bishop, Susan. "Should You Move Out of the Family Home During a Divorce?" www.divorcenet.com. April 15, 2013. https://www.divorcenet.com/resources/divorce/marital-property-division/should-you-move-out-family-hom

DiMaria, Lauren. "How Moving Can Trigger Depression in Children," Verywell Mind. Medically reviewed April 08, 2020 https://www.verywellmind.com/moving-depression-and-your-child-1066796

Selling the Home

How to Keep Your Home and Avoid Foreclosure | The Truth About Mortgage. "How to Keep Your Home and Avoid Foreclosure." Accessed on May 7, 2020. https://www.thetruthaboutmortgage.com/foreclosure-help/

Mortgage Calculators. "Talking to Your Kids About Losing Your Home: 4 Mistakes to Avoid." Accessed April 21, 2020. https://www.mortgagecalculators.info/resources/loss-of-home-guide-for-children.php

Foreclosure/Bankruptcy

Loftsgordon, Amy. "Foreclosure & Divorce." Www.nolo.com, Nolo, Updated 20 Feb. 2020, www.nolo.com/legal-encyclopedia/foreclosure-divorce.html.

Walker, Mandy. "Losing The Family Home." Since My Divorce. August 14, 2013. Retrieved from https://sincemydivorce.com/losing-the-family-home/

Brown, Suzy. "Selling A House During Divorce." Midlife Divorce Recovery. September 23, 2019. https://www.midlifedivorcerecovery.com/selling-a-house-during-divorce/

Chapter 6: Legal

Legal Process – Death
Shae Irving, J.D. NOLO. "Home Funeral Laws: An Overview". Accessed March 23, 2020. https://www.nolo.com/legal-encyclopedia/home-funeral-laws.html.

Legal Process-Divorce

"Divorce Series: How to File for Divorce". Divorce Series: How to File for Divorce | Maryland Courts. Accessed March 2, 2020. https://www.mdcourts.gov/video/selfhelp/divorce-series-how-file-divorce.

"Home". Maryland Legal Aid. Accessed March 2, 2020. https://www.mdlab.org/

"Maryland Courts Self-Help Center". Maryland Courts. Accessed March 2, 2020. https://mdcourts.gov/selfhelp/mcshc.

"Divorce". Divorce | Maryland Courts. Accessed March 2, 2020. https://www.mdcourts.gov/legalhelp/family/divorce.

Custody-Divorce

Maryland Courts. "Mediation & ADR." Accessed on April 28, 2020. https://mdcourts.gov/legalhelp/mediationadr.

Chapter 7: Finances

Insurance – Divorce

Logan, John. SafeGuard Guaranty. "Marriage Assurance". Accessed March 24, 2020. http://www.safeguardguaranty.com/

El-Sheikh, Sarah. "Egypt prepares draft law to oblige men to insure their ex-wives." Website Daily News Egypt. September 27, 2019. https://wwww.dailynewssegypt.com/2019/09/27/egypt-prepares-draft-law-to-oblige-men-to-insure-their-ex-wives/

Heath, Julia A. and B. F. Kiker. "Determinants of Spells of Poverty Following Divorce." Review of Social Economy. 50, no. 3 (1992). 305-315. https://doi.org/10.1080/758537075.

Wilkinson & Finkbeiner, LLP. "Divorce Statistics and Facts: What Affects Divorce Rates in the U.S.?" Accessed on April 28, 2020. https://www.wf-lawyers.com/divorce-statistics-and-facts/

Scafidi, Benjamin. The Taxpayers Costs of Divorce and Unwed Childbearing. PDF file. 2008. http://americanvalues.org/catalog/pdfs/COFF.pdf

Federal Assistance

Benefits Planner: Survivors | If You Are the Survivor | Social Security Administration. "Social Security." Accessed April 23, 2020. https://www.ssa.gov/planners/survivors/ifyou.html#h6

The Motley Fool. "3 Ways Children Can Get Social Security Benefits." June 3, 2016. https://www.fool.com/retirement/2016/06/03/3-ways-children-can-get-social-security-benefits.aspx

Medicaid. "Children's Health Insurance Program (CHIP)". Accessed February 20, 2020. https://www.medicaid.gov/chip/index.html

U.S. Department of Housing and Urban Development (HUD). "Office of Housing Choice Vouchers". Accessed January 09, 2020. https://www.hud.gov/program_offices/public_indian_housing/programs/hcv/about/fact_sheet

Divorce Costs

Maryland Courts. "Courts - Fee Schedules." Accessed March 23, 2020. https://mdcourts.gov/courts/feeschedules.

Maryland Courts. "Filing Fee Waivers." Accessed on April 28, 2020. https://mdcourts.gov/legalhelp/filingfeewaivers.

3stepdivorce.com: Premium Divorce Online. "3 Step Divorce - A Premium Online Divorce Solution. Accessed March 25, 2020. https://www.3stepdivorce.com/.

Maryland Courts. "Maryland Courts Self-Help Center". Accessed March 2, 2020. https://mdcourts.gov/selfhelp/mcshc.

Divorce | Maryland Courts. "Divorce". Accessed March 2, 2020. https://www.mdcourts.gov/legalhelp/family/divorce.

Maryland Courts. "Mediation & ADR." Accessed on April 28, 2020. https://mdcourts.gov/legalhelp/mediationadr

The People's Law Library of Maryland. "Divorce Mediation." Updated August 22, 2019. https://www.peoples-law.org/divorce-mediation

Questions on Family Mediation and Divorce Mediation in Maryland. "Maryland Divorce Mediation." Accessed April 23, 2020. https://www.mediate.com/NancyCaplan/pg3.cfm.

mdresolutioncenter. "Divorce Mediation Lawyer Howard County | Questions about Mediation | Baltimore Divorce Attorney". June 14, 2013, YouTube video. 7:38. https://www.youtube.com/watch?v=kSCakzqK8D4.

Martindale-Nolo Research. "How Much Does Divorce Cost in Maryland?" Lawyers.com. Accessed April 23, 2020. https://www.lawyers.com/legal-info/family-law/divorce/how-much-does-divorce-cost-in-maryland.html.

Religious Ramifications

Meyer, Cathy. "Getting an Annulment Through the Catholic Church". Mydomaine. January 16, 2020. https://www.mydomaine.com/how-to-obtain-an-annulment-through-the-catholic-church-1102452.

Yardley, Jim and Yardley and Elisabetta Povoledo. The New York Times. "Pope Francis Announces Changes for Easier Marriage Annulments" September 8, 2015. https://www.nytimes.com/2015/09/09/world/europe/pope-francis-marriage-annulment-reforms.html

Jewish Divorce, getting a get. "understanding the process of getting a get". Accessed January 30, 2020. http://www.getyourget.com/get-basics

Chapter 8: Faith

Christianity

BBC News. "What does Christianity say about marriage? - Marriage and divorce - GCSE Religious Studies Revision - BBC Bitesize." Accessed May 2, 2020. https://www.bbc.co.uk/bitesize/guides/z7w2fg8/revision/2

Islam

Denny, Frederick M. *Islam*. San Francisco: Harper San Francisco. 1987.

BBC News. "What does Islam say about marriage? - Marriage and divorce - GCSE Religious Studies Revision - BBC Bitesize." Accessed April 21, 2020. https://www.bbc.co.uk/bitesize/guides/zd8qn39/revision/2.

Huda. "Islamic Marriage Is a Legal Agreement, Known as Nikah." Learn Religions. February 11, 2020. https://www.learnreligions.com/definition-of-nikah-2004439.

Judaism

Lamm, Maurice. "The Jewish Way in Love and Marriage." New York: Jonathan David Publishers. 1991.

BBC News. "What does Judaism say about marriage? - Marriage and divorce - GCSE Religious Studies Revision – BBC Bitesize." Accessed on April 21, 2020. https://www.bbc.co.uk/bitesize/guides/zkkjpv4/revision/2

Christianity and Divorce

BBC News. "What does Christianity say about divorce and remarriage? - Marriage and divorce - GCSE Religious Studies Revision - BBC Bitesize." Accessed May 2, 2020. https://www.bbc.co.uk/bitesize/guides/z7w2fg8/revision/3

Islam and Divorce

BBC News. "What does Islam say about divorce and remarriage? - Marriage and divorce - GCSE Religious Studies Revision - BBC Bitesize." Accessed April 21, 2020. https://www.bbc.co.uk/bitesize/guides/zd8qn39/revision/3

Islamic Sharia. "Khula." March 13, 2017. http://www.islamic-sharia.org/khula/

Mir, Saima."Divorce, Islam and me: 'I will forever be the woman who left two husbands." The Guardian. February 16, 2019.
https://www.theguardian.com/lifeandstyle/2019/feb/16/divorce-islam-me-woman-who-left-two-husbands

Judaism and Divorce

BimBam. "How to Get a Jewish Divorce". November 17, 2015, YouTube video, 2:31.
https://www.youtube.com/watch?v=5kwuwVnNxGc

Real Stories. "Divorce: Jewish Style (Marriage Documentary) Real Stories". June 7, 2017, YouTube video, 51:39.
https://www.youtube.com/watch?v=TY0BPRczvNY

Jewish Divorce, getting a get. "Understanding the process of getting a get." Accessed April 8, 2020.
http://www.getyourget.com/get-basics

Encyclopedia Britannica. "Agunah". October 21, 2013.
https://www.britannica.com/topic/agunah

BBC News. "What does Judaism say about divorce and remarriage? Marriage and divorce - GCSE Religious Studies Revision - BBC Bitesize." Accessed April 21, 2020.
https://www.bbc.co.uk/bitesize/guides/zkkjpv4/revision/4

Chapter 9: Future

Friedman R. and J.W. James. *Moving On: Dump Your Relationship Baggage and Make Room for the Love of Your Life*. New York: M. Evans., 2006.

Kennedy Alexandria. *"Healing a broken heart after the loss of a loved one." Monterey Herald*, February 5, 2015.

https://www.montereyherald.com/2015/02/05/healing-a-broken-heart-after-the-loss-of-a-loved-one/

Merriam-Webster. "Dictionary by Merriam-Webster: America's most-trusted online dictionary." Accessed on April 2, 2020. http://www.merriam-webster.com/

The American Institute of Stress. *"Holmes-Rahe Stress Inventory."* April 10, 2019. http://www.stress.org/holmes-rahe-stress-inventory/

Take Time *and* Action to Grieve

James, J.W. and R. Friedman. *The Grief Recovery Handbook 20th Anniversary Edition.* Toronto: HarperCollins e-books, 2009

James, Allison. "3 Things You Shouldn't Do When Grieving a Divorce." The Grief Recovery Method. July 15, 2015. https://www.griefrecoverymethod.com/blog/2015/07/3-things-you-shouldnt-do-when-grieving-divorce.

Focus on Personal Growth

Shaw Gina "After Divorce: 8 Tips for Reinventing Yourself." WebMD. April 27, 2012. https://www.webmd.com/sex-relationships/features/life-after-divorce#1

Get Help for Your Kids

Oprah.com. "Valerie Bertinelli Comes Clean" February 25, 2008. https://www.oprah.com/oprahshow/valerie-bertinelli-comes-clean/all

Seek Follow-up Legal Help

Wong Brittany. "The First Thing You Must Do When Your Divorce Is Final." Huffpost. October 2, 2017. https://www.huffpost.com/entry/8-things-you-should-do-when-your-divorce-is-final_n_57b768d6e4b0b51733a38119?utm_hp_ref=divorce-advice

Afterword

Johnson, Mel. GodUpdates. "A Mom Shares Her Story of Love After Divorce". December 4, 2017. https://www.godupdates.com/love-after-divorce-kristina-kuzmic/

Kuzmic, Kristina. "Don't Settle". Kristina Kuzmic, November 30, 2017. YouTube video, 4:40. https://www.youtube.com/watch?v=KUEDImzAjSg.

ABOUT THE AUTHOR

Stanley McCluskey grew up in Alabama with his mom, dad, and three younger brothers. When he was twenty years old his parents divorced and he learned first-hand the phrase that a divorced friend had uttered to him two years prior, "divorce is worse than death."

Everyone dies but everyone does not necessarily divorce, and Stanley never imagined that divorce would happen to his family. It broke his heart, especially when he looked around at friends whose families were still intact. *Why his family?* Even years later when he had the unfortunate task of burying his parents on separate occasions, the pain he felt with their deaths paled in comparison to the pain that he still feels today when he thinks of the divorce.

During his life, he has found that on several occasions that, when talking to a friend going through a divorce who seemed depressed, distracted and numb, when he shared that "divorce is worse than death," their countenance would change with relief as if someone understood—and he wanted to share this book to share that hope, strength and relief with others.

Stanley resides in Ellicott City, Maryland and enjoys spending time with his family, reading, and riding "Sporty," his Harley Davidson Sportster motorcycle. Yes, his wife is a saint; she let him keep Sporty after his accident.

Made in the USA
Middletown, DE
27 August 2020